SOCIAL MEDIA MUSINGS

GEORGE WAAS

authorHOUSE®

AuthorHouse™
1663 Liberty Drive
Bloomington, IN 47403
www.authorhouse.com
Phone: 833-262-8899

Published by AuthorHouse 02/26/2022

ISBN: 978-1-6655-5313-1 (sc)
ISBN: 978-1-6655-5314-8 (e)

Library of Congress Control Number: 2022903789

Print information available on the last page.

CONTENTS

this from former Harvard President Derek Bok, "if you think education is expensive, try ignorance."

For the most part, however, I pretty much kept my opinions to myself, or shared them with family and friends, until January 6, 2021 when for the first time since 1812, our nation's Capital came under siege as a mass of Trump supporters tried to stop the constitutionally required certification of the Electoral College vote for the next president of the United States.

Since then, taking to heart the note on the Facebook page that says "What's on your mind," I've posted on Facebook my thoughts and opinions about various situations. Many of my posts are quite lengthy, solely because of the importance I place on analysis, fact, reason, logic, critical thinking and sound judgment.

What follows in chronological order from January 6, 2021 to February, 2022 are posts on a variety of subjects, mostly— but certainly not all— on politics. If nothing else, we need a national dialog on issues of great public importance. And we need that dialog to begin yesterday. Here is my take.

"WHAT ARE WE SUPPOSED TO DO?"

"What are we supposed to do?" This was the memorable statement made by one of the rioters during the siege on our nation's Capital on January 6. This rioter said further: "The Supreme Court won't help us. Congress won't help us." So, he reasoned, it was up to him and his ilk to take the law into their own hands and, following Trump and his acolytes, take over the government of the United States and thereby supplant law with anarchy. However, so far, I've not been able to find anyone who answered his basic question. So, here's my take. In our Democracy, when there is a challenge to a law, the courts are the final arbiter. When the judiciary, in more than 60 cases including two at the Supreme Court, uniformly rejected every claim of a rigged election, supporters of Democracy don't have to agree with the courts' decisions, but they have to accept them. And this is where the rioters are so obviously wrong and wrongheaded.

It's not up to them to choose to accept lie after lie about a rigged election, even if these lies are fueled by those who have taken an oath to support the Constitution of the United States and oppose all enemies, foreign and domestic. As was done in 2000, although many didn't agree with the Supreme Court's decision that awarded George Bush the presidency, we who support Democracy were obligated to accept it. And we did. If each one of us were free to disregard the actions of our government and pursue our ends as we saw fit, choosing with impunity to believe whatever we chose to believe, we would replace Democracy with anarchy. We can only hope that what happened on January 6 is not repeated. And we must expect those elected officials who fed these mindless minions with repeated lies are held accountable for aiding and abetting an armed insurrection.

Those who stormed the capitol must be also be held accountable for their seditious actions. It is accountability that provides guardrails protective of our Democracy. What happened was not a peaceful protest or demonstration protected by the First Amendment; it was a direct violent assault on our form of government. May our better angels prevail, and may the strength of our Democracy overcome this act of insurrection.

QANON AND THE TWILIGHT ZONE

Last night, CNN broadcast a special on QAnon. As I watched, what amazed me was how easy it is to sway the minds of the gullible; those who willingly fall prey to the power of suggestion, regardless of how outlandishly devoid of logic, reason and common sense. And I recalled that great TV series of the 1960s, **The Twilight Zone.** I'm sure many of you are familiar with this series; episodes are now shown on the SciFi network during certain holiday periods. It has been said that its creator, Rod Serling, had a keen sense of human nature and the human experience. He began each episode with an opening narrative. One such narrative struck me as most relevant to the QAnon movement. Some of you might recall it: "It is the middle ground between light and shadow, between science and superstition, and it lies between the pit of man's fears and the summit of his knowledge. This is the dimension of imagination. It is an area which we call the Twilight Zone." I emphasize the key language because I believe it expresses precisely what drives the current iteration of extremism. Shadow, superstition and fear. And if you can tap into that, you can motivate and control. There was one particular episode out of the more than 150 that comprise the Twilight Zone collection, and ranks as one of the most popular episodes. It's entitled "The Monsters are Due on Maple Street." Those of you who are Twilight Zone fans well remember this one; those who are not familiar are encouraged to check it out on YouTube.

Without getting into details, substitute the source of misinformation in that episode, with an entity that stands to benefit the most by sowing today's right-wing extremism, and you get the idea of how easy it is to turn friend against friend, and neighbor against neighbor. In this TZ episode, it was the flashing of lights, a few unexplained sounds, and before long, well, the result was violence. Serling understood the frailties and weaknesses of human nature, and his many episodes dealt with manifestations of that keen understanding. Today, social media, where just about anything goes, feed suggestibility and psychic vulnerability. The wilder the story, the most cryptic of messages, the most outlandish of allegations, serve as rocket fuel for extremism of the most dangerous kind. But it's not as if this is new.

Recall the Weimar Republic, which governed Germany following World War I and ruled from 1919-1933.

The founders of the Weimar Republic, Jews, socialists, liberals, war profiteers, and others on the home front were blamed for undermining the war effort. Enter Adolf Hitler, and we know what followed. We know that our republic requires eternal vigilance if it is to survive. In the past, each generation, when faced with an existential crisis, made it through the storm through the efforts of our better angels. We must call upon our better angels to deal with our current crisis of conscience. Find those who are planting the seeds of anger and discontent in the minds of the gullible. Follow the funding sources. Is the enemy homegrown? Is it fueled from foreign soil? Reason, logic, common sense, rationality must prevail. The alternative is simply inconceivable.

COVID'S CONSEQUENCES

This headline, **"Some May Not Recover Senses"** which appears in today's USA Today, caught my eye. The article is about those who suffered from COVID-19, recovered, but did not recover some of their senses. We know of reports of virus victims losing their senses of smell and taste. However, researchers aren't sure whether they will ever recover their senses; only time will tell. But there is one sense that too many others have lost, and it doesn't look as if they will ever recover this lost sense.

It is the sense that has been demonstrably lost by those who incited and encouraged the attack on our capitol on January 6; by those who carried out the seditious assault; those who gave aid and comfort to the rioters during and after the attack; and those who continue to ignore or excuse the inexcusable, even giving aid to a member of Congress who has called for the murder of her fellow representatives with whom she disagrees. That sense that appears irretrievably lost is common sense. Common sense is defined by Merriam-Webster as, "sound and prudent judgment based on a simple perception of the situation or facts."

Thus, "common sense" equates to the knowledge and experience which most people already have, or which the person using the term believes that they do or should have. It isn't necessarily based on education level; it's derived from the accumulation of life's knowledge from youth to adulthood, and life experiences. Common sense is what we generally rely on when making decisions. Common sense factors into deciding right from wrong. Take those who precipitated January 6 (a new day in our nation's history that will go down in infamy).

Did Donald Trump use common sense when he repeatedly lied about the election? How about when he urged his followers to attack the Capitol? Did his loyal sycophants in Congress use common sense when they repeated the "rigged election" lie and either remained silent or supported the rioters? How about that member of Congress who refuses to disavow her threats to other members, and those

THE GRAND OLD PARTY IS NO MORE

While we were appalled at the attempted coup of our nation's government on January 6, we have already witnessed a coup: the takeover of the Republican Party by radical right-wing extremists. The Grand Old Party is no more. The party of Lincoln, and later Reagan and the Bushes, is gone. Do you think this takeover has eluded Florida? Where is the outrage at the January 6 madness from Gov. DeSantis and Senators Rubio and Scott? How about the leadership of the state's Republican Party? If you can find their condemnation of Trump's incitement speech, the assault on the Capitol, and the vast majority of Republican members of Congress who are critical of Trump, by all means please post them on this page.

The Republican senators wrap themselves in the Constitution by claiming that Trump's impeachment is unconstitutional, but they remain curiously silent about his unconstitutional incitement, and the unconstitutional acts of his followers. The Republican Party (I can no longer refer to it as the GOP, because today's party is alien to the Grand Old Party) is now the party of Trump, Cruz, Hawley, Greene, and their wild-eyed ilk. For them, lying, excusing criminal behavior from the right, and adhering to baseless conspiracies is the norm. It's past time to ask that party members admit to the great lie of a stolen election, condemn the criminal activity that we saw on live TV, and take the party back to its roots of limited government, individual freedom and less taxation. This should have happened immediately. But, like the Cowardly Lion in the Wizard of Oz, they all lost their courage; they have no nerve. (Following this analogy, they also show no heart, and no brains.)

So, what are the few Republicans who have spoken out to do? They must either choose to remain in the now properly renamed Retrumpican Party, or become independents, or join the ranks of the Democrats. This is the choice that has been foisted upon them. Let us see if there are Republicans who have courage, the heart to do the right thing to protect our democracy, and the brains to deal with what has happened to the GOP.

FOOLS AND DANGEROUS FOOLS

There are fools and there are fools who pose a serious threat to Democracy. Fortunately, the former can be dealt with far easier than the latter. History shows that governing, except in major crises like war and depression, takes place in the center, or as close to the center as circumstances demand. Lincoln temporarily assumed wide powers during the Civil War, as did FDR during the early years of his first term, and during his third term--depression and war years. Now, we face a pandemic, and Biden will need every vote in the Senate to move us toward ending the pandemic, especially since so little was done previously. I don't excuse the fools on the left, but I am far more concerned about the fools on the right. We elect officials to provide the leadership necessary to preserve our democratic republic. And we

CHECKING BIAS VS. REAL NEWS

I am not at all surprised at those who watch Fox News. I think the more information you seek, the better you are at what you do. Narrowness of mind is not the quality of a good news reporter. There are two professions that require digging for facts, journalism and law. And I'm proud to have been involved in both. And narrowness of mind doesn't make for a good lawyer, either. But getting the facts isn't easy; folks want to spin them for their own benefit, and documents can be prepared by people with an agenda. Again, separating the wheat from the chaff. But once you have the facts, it is then permissible to offer an opinion on them, so long as the viewer is made aware of this distinction. Presenting facts without opinion is contrary to human nature; we are emotional creatures. But this separation is what makes our tasks difficult, and it takes training and experience to successfully accomplish this.

IF ONLY THE DEMOCRATS COULD GO IT ALONE

After yesterday's House vote on the 1.9 trillion COVID stimulus bill, it should be painfully obvious that the Democrats must go it alone. Simply put, they are wasting their time trying to get any cooperation from the latest iteration of the Republican Party. That House vote, largely along party lines (two Democrats defected—something that the Democratic Congressional Campaign Committee should remind these two when they ask for campaign funds for 2022) should send a loud and clear message that the Republicans will do nothing to advance the promises President Biden made during last year's campaign.

The Senate is no different. Why should the Republican senators act any differently? There is nothing in it for them if they do anything to make Biden look good. The Republicans will continue to rail away at what he and his administration does or doesn't do. Never mind the lies; ignore January 6, ignore how they handled the pandemic. Just keep on screaming about Socialism, conservative values, and other lines in the Republican emotive grab bag, and hope the voters don't remember, or ask what specific values they are talking about.

As long as Biden has the narrow majority in the Senate, he should advance as many of his campaign promises as he can, and continue to inform the electorate about Republican obstructionism. (And if any Democrats defect, just remind them the next time they seek funds from the Democratic Senatorial Campaign Committee. Hear that, Sen. Manchin?)

In the meantime, President Biden should continue to reach out to the voters directly, as he did during his recent visit to Texas. He bumped hands with the governor—certainly no friend to the president—and met with community leaders and the voters. Hopefully, those voters, come election time, will remember who was there for them in their time of need. Ignore the party, go for the minds and hearts of the voters. And if some Republicans want to join hands, all the better. But he should simply prepare for the Democrats to go it alone.

Nowhere is the Republican Party's distain for anything Biden more evident than in the several states where Republican legislators are busy re-writing election laws, using the tiresome and baseless claim of eliminating voter fraud. They will continue this line ad nauseam, and do it with a straight face, but they are fooling only those who are willing to be fooled, or too ignorant to know otherwise.

These Republican legislators are buying into the Big Lie of a rigged election. Never mind that they make no such claim for congressional, senatorial, gubernatorial, or state legislative elections. No, for them, only the presidential election was rigged. How so? More than 60 judges unanimously said not so. But to foment the Big Lie, that doesn't matter. The courts are just part of the conspiracy. Even those appointed by Trump.

Just yesterday, at the CPAC meeting in Orlando, Gov. Ron DeSantis, in praising Florida's handling of the pandemic, probably made a telling slip of the tongue when he said that last year's election went off without a hitch. If he really means that, why the need for "reform" legislation? Especially when the use of this word is a subterfuge for suppression? Someone undoubtedly has already told him to get back on message.

Here is what the Democrats must be prepared to do as soon as this legislation is signed by the Republican governors. First, voting is not a privilege; it is a right protected by the United States Constitution. Proof: The Fifteenth, Nineteenth and Twenty-sixth Amendments say so in unmistakably clear language. The Fifteenth (dealing with race, color or previous condition of servitude) and Nineteenth (sex discrimination) both begin with these same 10 words: "The **right** of citizens of the United States **to vote**...". The Nineteenth (18 years of age) says "The **right** of citizens of the United States....**to vote**... ."

Second, this right to vote, particularly when considered with the First Amendment's freedom of speech, the right to peacefully assemble, and the right to petition the government for redress of grievances, is a fundamental right, which means it is a right recognized by the Supreme Court as requiring a high degree of protection from government encroachment. Rights specifically identified in the Constitution, and even those under the Due Process Clause, are considered fundamental.

This means that, subject to certain uniform procedural steps (usually couched as time, place or manner), fundamental rights cannot be restricted or diminished in any way. (Parenthetically, it is noted that Congress has recognized the right to vote in the 1965 Voting Rights Act.)

Having established that the right to vote is a fundamental right founded in our Constitution, laws and Supreme billion, 11. Jim Walton - $62.1 billion, 12. Rob Walton - $61.8 billion, 13. MacKenzie Scott - $57 billion, 14. Michael Bloomberg - $55 billion, 15. Charles Koch - $45 billion. The total from these 15 multibillionaires alone tops one trillion dollars.

America's population is around 340 million. The top 1% of Americans—or 3.4 million--have a combined net worth of $34.2 trillion, according to Federal Reserve data last updated Oct. 19, 2020. That number represents more than 30% of all household wealth in the U.S. To be in that rarefied atmosphere of wealth, the floor for household earnings is $531,000; for individuals the sum is $361,000.

Contrast this with the 34 million at or below the poverty level (in 2019); that is, an income of $26,200 per year or less for a family of four in 2020); approximately 53 percent of Americans—and 78 percent of workers--say they live from paycheck to paycheck.

To say that there is wealth inequality in America is to state the obvious. At this point, the right wing of our political spectrum will undoubtedly shout that they know where this is going, and a redistribution of the wealth is Communism, Socialism, anti-American, punishing the hard-working rich, rewarding the slovenly poor, etc., etc., etc.

But consider this. How did the superrich actually earn their wealth? Was it all hard work, or did they have at least some help from government? What about those tax breaks that are unique to the wealthy? Isn't that a form of welfare, corporate welfare? If the tax system allows a superrich (assuming accuracy) former president to pay no taxes for several years, and only $750 in one year, and certain retirees pay over $15,000 in taxes, what does this say about tax equity? Compare what you pay in taxes each year with what the superrich pay. Are you satisfied with this tax system?

Now for the sake of discussion, here's an example. If that that 3.4 million who make up the top 1% were taxed just 5% of their accumulated $34 trillion, that would generate revenue of $1.7 trillion annually…or allow for an annual stimulus check.

And what would people do with this stimulus money? Keep reading.

My next question. Would any of these individuals miss that 5%? Would they have to move to a smaller house? Perhaps sell one or more of their other residences? Would they purchase fewer cars? Have less food on their tables? Have to sell off any of their possessions? Take fewer vacations? Cut back on their social lives? Of course not. They wouldn't miss a penny of it.

But some in this small but powerful group say that if they are required to pay more in taxes, they will hide their assets. Of course, changes in our tax laws will prevent this.

In stark contrast, a graphic reality about those workers living from paycheck to paycheck. Remember, while the

10 years. Redistricting is how districts are created once population figures are determined following the decennial census. All seats must be as near to population equality as possible. Over the years, technology has made the population variances among districts almost non-existent.) The party in power in the legislature controls the redistricting process for both congressional and state legislative seats. Remember the first rule of politics is survival; the second is perpetuation.

1992 was the first time the Supreme Court standard for dealing with the creation of representative districts was addressed following the 1982 Supreme Court decision and 1990 reapportionment and redistricting. Although not specifically authorized by judicial decision, Democrats and national voting rights groups like the People for the American Way, the Brennan Center for Justice and the League of United Latin American Citizens, maintained that to the extent a majority/minority district can be created, states were obligated to do so. (A majority/minority district is one that is generally majority populated by a minority group.) Minority groups advocated support for these districts, believing they were entitled to representation that was denied them by the system then in place.

The plans that were circulated in the legislature (congressional seats and state legislative seats are established by state legislatures) sought to accomplish this goal by packing as many minorities into as many districts as possible that created putatively lawful minority/majority districts.

While this had the effect of creating relatively safe—albeit few—minority/majority districts, the surrounding districts necessarily lost those minority leaning voters.

The Republicans saw this as an opportunity because if you pack democratic voters in a few districts, the effect is to bleach surrounding districts, making the voting populace in them whiter and Republican. And this is precisely what happened in 1992 and beyond. Since the 1990s, Florida's legislature has been majority Republican, and the last Democrat Governor was Lawton Chiles; Florida has not elected a Democrat governor this century.

Now for a brief word on single-member districts. Before our current single-member districts for legislative seats, we had multi-member districts. For example, Dade County might have five senators, each of whom ran countywide. This means you had to broaden your appeal to different interests in order to get elected in multi-member districts. To the contrary, single-member districts, because of their size and focus on narrower issues, allow for more single-issue legislators. Prior to the 1990s, Florida legislators could serve as long as the voters sent them to Tallahassee.

But in the 1990s, the state Constitution was amended to provide for term limits--eight years for the Senate (two terms) and eight years for the House (four terms). When coupled with single-member districts, the result is legislators who are more apt to be single-issue short-timers who are looking more at advancing politically than becoming long-term legislators with institutional knowledge. And many of these legislators wind up elected governors, members of Congress, and state cabinet officials. You get the picture.

And this, in my view, generally explains in some measure how we got to where we are today.

True colors. This refers to the kind of person someone really is rather than what the person seems to be. Sooner or later, people show their true colors. This applies most graphically to those who make up the dominant far-right iteration of the Republican Party.

REPUBLICANS ARE GOOD AT PLAYING THE EMOTION CARD

In recent years, the Republican Party has been wildly successful in using emotion-driven sound bites in their political campaigns. When you hear the party faithful recite the party mantra: "family values," "less taxes," and "less government," the natural reaction is that those who oppose these "policy issues" are against family values and favor more taxes and big government, the latter evoking the image of intrusion into one's everyday life. The latter slides into their old familiar refrain of "Socialism" they repeatedly and largely successfully attach to any program that they don't like because it intrudes on freedom (corporate freedom, that is) and wealth accumulation at the top of the economic food chain. They use these emotive blasts to conjure up a loss of freedom and individuality, precisely the intended result the right wing wants. And when there is violence, they add "radical left-wing extremists" or the latest-- "Antifa"--to the mix.

They know well that to fully understand what these sound bites actually mean requires critical thinking. And that's something the GOP hopes you won't use, instead going no further than a purely and fully emotional reaction driven by these sound bites. The Republican Party depends on folks who have no long-term memory.

Just ask Ted Cruz.

But under an even cursory analysis, their sound bites don't match performance. And this is where their true colors are shown.

First, family values. When you hear that phrase, you naturally think of God, country, the American Flag, family, and other feel-good subjects. But you must not go any further; you must not ask how the party can justify supporting an adulterous, narcissistic, pathological liar who denigrates science in favor of ideology, and who rails against our nation's allies while currying favor with dictators and tyrants. You must not lay blame for January 6 on the instigator-in-chief. You must not think about how his vocal supporters attacked law enforcement officers on that fateful day. There are certainly other examples, but how these specific ones exemplify family values remains unanswered.

representatives hope the people won't notice their true colors. Most do, however.

The current version of the Republican Party is not the party of Lincoln, Theodore Roosevelt, Dwight Eisenhower, Ronald Reagan or even George Bush I and II. All that is necessary to see the party's true colors is to avoid reacting to their emotion-charged rhetoric, and put on your critical thinking caps.

THE REPUBLICAN CHANT TO ANY INCREASE IN TAXES

President Biden will soon propose a tax increase, the first major overhaul of the tax code since the 1980s. (The 2017 so-called tax overhaul reduced the corporate tax rate from 35% to 21% and overwhelmingly benefitted wealthy shareholders and highly paid executives. Small individual tax cuts are set to expire in 2025; those for the wealthy are permanent.) Already, we can hear the Republicans rant about "just another liberal tax-and-spend program that takes money from you and gives it to the undeserved"--- hoping you will get so emotionally distraught, you won't bother yourself with those pesky things called facts. But here are the facts about the Biden plan:

Raising the corporate tax rate to 28% from 21%;

Paring back tax preferences for so-called pass-through businesses, such as limited-liability companies or partnerships;

Raising the income tax rate on individuals earning more than $400,000;

Expanding the estate tax's reach;

A higher capital-gains tax rate for individuals earning at least $1 million annually. Do you see anything here that will affect your taxes? And what will the revenue raised from this proposal be used for? Three major things: infrastructure, climate and expanded help for poorer Americans. The next time you blow out a tire driving over a huge pothole, ask yourself whether infrastructure repair and maintenance are important to you, especially since you are most likely not going to pay for them. The next time extreme weather impacts your life--flooding along our coast, tornados and hurricanes of unprecedented strength decimating your property--or that of a loved one or friend--ask whether taking action to deal with climate change is important enough to you, again since you are most likely not going to pay for it. On the final point, whether or not you favor aiding poorer Americans, that there is income and expenditure inequality in America is a fact. Just read up on the history of zoning patterns, called "redlining." The adage of "the rich get richer, and the poor get poorer" is a truism. Now, before the predictable cries of "government handout," remember our tax code favors the wealthy.

They didn't accumulate wealth solely by the sweat of their brow; they had help by advantageous tax cuts and deductions available to no one else; frequently called "corporate welfare." And, once again, since your taxes most likely won't go up one farthing, are you opposed to seeing poorer Americans given help--especially if you own a business and depend on purchasing power to remain in business? Remember, what do people do when they have more money? They either spend or save it.

By spending, they create greater demand, which means businesses have to increase supply. And how do businesses do this? By hiring more people and producing more-- which in turn increases purchasing power. And if they save, this means banks and other lending institutions have more money to lend for investment purposes--which also increases purchasing power. This is known as the great economic cycle. So, when Biden proposes his tax plan, and the Republicans launch their predictable diatribe, let the facts direct your opinion, not emotion.

WHO REALLY BELIEVES THAT THE VOTING RESTRICTIONS ARE REFORM MEASURES?

If the DOJ takes action against these "reform" measures, it will be up to the judiciary to decide the outcome. And this is where Mitch McConnell's efforts at reshaping the courts come into play. One-fourth of all federal judges are Trump appointees; three are on the Supreme Court. Six of the nine justices are conservative, and they are not favorably disposed to the Voting Rights Act. These legislators are banking on the judiciary to defer to them. The recently argued Arizona case looks like it will be a strong indicator of how the courts will look at voting changes in the future. Upon to now, any change from an existing provision that restricted access to voting, was considered a violation. The Court, however, has signaled that this may no longer be the law. And once some restrictions are permitted, the law becomes a slippery slope regarding future "reforms."

ACADEMIC FREEDOM IS JUST THOUGHT CONTROL FOR FLORIDA REPUBLICANS

Florida Republican legislators are supporting bills requiring students and faculty at state public universities to identify political bias in college classrooms. This would include allowing students to record their instructor's lectures. Evidently, Republicans are concerned that university faculty members generally lean left on the political scale. Never mind the specter of government Thought Police in the classroom, I don't believe these Republicans are not asking the right question. That is, why do college faculty lean left? The broader question is why do highly educated people tend to lean left?

Carl Cassidy, former Senior International Executive Fortune 500 company, offers a lengthy, heavily researched article on this very subject, a part of which is quoted here.

"There is a direct and positive correlation between intelligence and the degree of education reached, the more intelligent the greater the probability of being able to advance to a higher level of education. So, it's no surprise that highly educated people are smarter. "It's a well-worn (if not-entirely-agreed-upon) idea that college makes people more liberal. And a fairly recent 2016 Pew study reports that to be the case. Pew reports that most educated Americans have grown increasingly liberal over the last couple of decades." Source: Why Are Highly Educated Americans Getting More Liberal?"

A report from the Pew Research Center finds a wide partisan gap between highly educated and non-highly-educated Americans. Not only that, but the share of college grads and post-graduates who are "consistently liberal" (based on their answers to a series of policy questions) has grown sharply in the last 20 years." Source: Why Are Highly Educated Americans Getting More Liberal?

"Split it out by party, and the shift is even starker. Among the post-grad set, "more than half of Democrats and Democratic-leaners today are "consistently liberal," up from fewer than one-in-five in 1994. Likewise, among college grads, it jumped from 12 to 47."

This squares with something Pew found: "while the partisan identification of people without college degrees have held steady over the last couple of decades, people with college degrees increasingly identify as Democratic or lean that way". Source: A Deep Dive Into Party Affiliation

"There's some pretty good evidence that going to college leads people to have more liberal attitudes on social issues, in particular on issues of tolerance, of difference and issues of gender equity," said Neil Gross, sociology professor at Colby College, who has studied liberalism at colleges. Intelligence, Personality, and Interests in the Career Choice Process - Phillip L. Ackerman, Margaret E. Beier, 2003

"We've known for a while that people with more education tend to be more ideologically consistent than people with less education," he said. "In some sense it's not surprising to see that polarization and party sorting is happening most among people who are super highly educated." A Deep Dive Into Party Affiliation Source: Intelligence, Personality, and Interests in the Career Choice Process - Phillip L. Ackerman, Margaret E. Beier, 2003

"Although education plays a big factor in producing liberal-minded people, we are also a product of our environment, and educated people are influenced by environment, which brings up the ongoing argument of what has more influence, genes or environment? Although social scientists agree that both have influence, it is accepted that as we age, leave home and experience life this environmental flexibility gives us the opportunity to adjust to changes as we are influenced to a greater degree based on what we learn and experiences we encounter. Conservatives often complain that liberals control the media, show business or academia or some other social institutions. The Hypothesis explains why conservatives are correct in their complaints. Liberals do control the media, or show business, or academia, among other institutions, because, apart from a few areas in life (such as business) where countervailing circumstances may prevail, liberals control all institutions. They control the institutions because liberals are on average more intelligent than conservatives and thus they are more likely to attain the highest status in any area of modern life," "A Deep Dive Into Party Affiliation

I also posit that because intelligent people are motivated to learn, travel, experience new situations, and cultures, they are naturally attracted to that end of the spectrum that engages the brain and challenges the intellect, not so much the physical. So logically, it follows that these people end up with degrees and professions in academia, the media, social and governmental institutions that demand intelligence and learning.

So, turning to politics, can we draw any conclusions in terms of how the two major American political parties stack up. I believe, what we have seen over the last 25 to 30 years gives us some very decided insights, (although antidotally I will agree) as to their collective intelligence. My take is that the Republican party is most decidedly the "Dumb Party" attracting and putting up with the right-wing lunatic fringe and electing members who are decidedly short in terms of simple brain power and common knowledge. The GOP run and elect members to Congress that believe women can't get pregnant from rape if they "will" the pregnancy to be avoided, and believe that global warming is a hoax, and Trump their esteemed leader has suggested on more than one occasion that Hurricanes could be eradicated if only we were to nuke them. ...

Conservative political ideologies tend to be associated with lower intelligence on average. Conservatives generally value tradition, respect for authority, and social order, and tend to be leery of innovation and change. These scholars have argued that such values tend to be associated with cognitive rigidity and may therefore appeal to people who have difficulty with intellectual challenges that require them to process novel information. In support of this, Stankov (2009) cited evidence that people with more conservative views tend to score lower on IQ tests and to have lower levels of education." Source: Intelligence And Politics Have a Complex Relationship"

His point is that if the conservative viewpoint is to gain traction in our colleges and universities, it will have to rely on competence, wisdom and critical thinking to meet the challenge in the marketplace of ideas. Attending college is a voluntary act; society doesn't force anyone to enroll. In college, students learn, among other things, which political party has done the most to promote the health, safety and well-being for society as a whole. Social Security, Medicare, Medicaid, workers' compensation, unemployment compensation, civil rights, voting rights--you get the idea.

Emotive sound bites, wild theories, claims without evidence, repeated lies, etc., simply won't cut it--no matter how many surveys are conducted under this draconian legislation.

I SUPPOSE THIS JUDGE NEVER HEARD OF RIGHT-WING BIAS

The recent headline screams: Federal Judge Laurence Silberman slams media, accusing it of left-wing bias.

The newspaper article says "A federal appeals judge accused the media of being a "trumpet" for the Democratic Party in a scathing dissenting opinion handed down Friday. Washington, DC, Senior Circuit Judge Laurence Silberman, 85, called on his fellow judges to overturn a Supreme Court landmark decision protecting the press, complaining that conservatives are oppressed by liberal outlets, academia and tech companies that combine to create "a frighteningly orthodox media culture."

Nowhere in his opinion, however, does the judge ask the obvious question: why do media outlets lean to the left on the political scale? Also left unanswered by the judge's diatribe is another obvious question: assuming the country is divided roughly 50-50 as many believe it is, if the demand is that the liberal media become more conservative, shouldn't conservative media strive to become more liberal, in the name of fair and balanced reporting?

What the judge is actually referring to is political reporting; news reports on car crashes, armed robbery arrests, high school graduations, etc., hardly implicate matters of political bias. But it is one thing to criticize the media for being biased; it's quite another to determine causes, and effect remediation.

One response to the question of bias comes from a lengthy Washington Post article that is summarized below. As you read this response, ask yourself whether it's the media's fault, or does the fault lie with the audience, or elsewhere? And is it actually a matter of fault, or one of preferences? The analysis below informs that believing the issue can be resolved by demanding that the liberal media become more conservative is far too simplistic in that it fails to take into account big-market geography, educational level and background, and the journalist's crusader zeal.

The report begins by declaring "that characterization of mainstream media newsrooms as left-leaning indeed has documentary backing.

"The Pew Research Center in 2004 undertook a nationwide survey of 547 local and national reporters, editors and executives. The result? Thirty-four percent of national press identified as liberal, as opposed to 7 percent conservative ("moderate" was the largest category). Liberal identification among national press types had shot up from 22 percent in 1995.

The American Society of News Editors does an annual diversity survey, but it doesn't probe this particular incarnation, according to executive director Teri Hayt. "Diversity is more than gender or race," writes Hayt in an email. "It's more important than ever before that news organizations reflect their communities if they want to provide a consistent fair and balanced news report. News organizations must do better with women and minorities in leadership and reporting positions and just as important, they must have diverse opinions within the news operation to have a meaningful conversation around coverage." (And how will increasing diversity impact news coverage? Will this make coverage more conservative?)

"The granddaddy of research on this topic is "The American Journalist," a series of studies that dates to the 1970s. In 2006, the series found that journalists had edged a bit to the right over the preceding decade but that newsrooms still skewed more lefty than the U.S. population at large. ... A 2014 study under the "American Journalist" banner found that 28 percent of 1,080 surveyed U.S. journalists claimed to be Democrats, as opposed to 7 percent for Republicans. The numbers reflected a desertion of both parties toward a self-identification as independent, which clocked in at 50 percent of the surveyed population.

Tim Graham, executive editor of NewsBusters, has a different take: "Journalists have gotten incredibly reluctant to identify with a party. I suspect liberals check the 'independent' box to avoid being properly identified."

Its parent organization, the Media Research Center, has published a massive roundup of research on the political leanings of U.S. newsrooms. As Graham sees it, the data in some cases understates the tilt in mainstream media newsrooms, with significant ramifications for governance.

"Though the Grahams ... may dispute emphases, data over the years confirms the contentions of American conservatives that the workplaces of the mainstream media err on the liberal/Democratic side of the ideological/partisan divide. "I think over the years that we've done these studies, it's clear that more journalists tend to lean to the left politically than to the right," says retired Indiana University journalism professor David H. Weaver. How'd that happen?

1) **The geographical explanation**. The hulking organs of the mainstream media reside in New York, Washington and other metropolises, where liberals live on top of other liberals. The residency pattern of these big-time reporters and editors quite consistently overlaps with the blue-coded areas of the country that voted for Hillary Clinton, who won the District of Columbia with 91 percent of the vote. A July 2004 column by then-New York Times Public Editor Daniel Okrent conveys the best articulation of this concept: "Today, only 50 percent of The Times's readership resides in metropolitan New York, but the paper's heart, mind and habits remain embedded here. You can take the paper out of the city, but without an effort to take the city and all its attendant provocations, experiments and attitudes out of

the paper, readers with a different worldview will find The Times an alien beast," wrote Okrent in a story titled, "Is The New York Times a Liberal Newspaper?" The answer from Okrent: "Of course it is."

Cosmopolitan influences even seep into a fortress like right-leaning Fox News, according to Joe Muto, the onetime "Fox News mole" who wrote a book — "An Atheist in the Foxhole" — about his attempts to leak insider-y scoops from the network. Though the upper ranks of Fox News management were filled with committed conservatives, there was no uniformity down low. "People outside of Fox tended to assume that the whole building was filled with lockstep conservatives, but at a certain point, it was simply impossible to staff a business based in New York City, and consisting of people who were attracted to the field of journalism, without letting at least a few pinkos in," wrote Muto in his book.

2) **The crusader explanation**. Tracy Grant, deputy managing editor of The Washington Post, is familiar with criticisms about the composition of newsrooms — she handles recruitment and diversity at the newspaper. Asked about studies showing a lefty tilt, she tells this blog: "I think people are called to this profession sometimes have a sense of mission about shining light in dark places," she says. "I think there is a sensibility among people who feel that calling and if there is a commonality of people who go into journalism, it is people inspired by things like Watergate or 'Spotlight' — that idea of telling stories that need to

be told and so that does represent a little bit of rooting for the underdog mentality, but I also think that anybody who thinks that the mainstream media — the Washington Post — didn't make Hillary Clinton's life miserable or Barack Obama's life miserable by holding them the accountable is just not looking at the record."

"3) **The school-tie explanation**. The pipeline for hiring decisions at big media outlets files through elite colleges that crank out lefty students, maintains NewsBusters' Graham. "I'm a good example of the how to not get hired at a national news organization, considering my background," says Graham, <u>a 1986 graduate of Bemidji State University in Bemidji, Minn</u>. There he founded and edited the conservative Bemidji Student Review. He started at the Media Research Center in 1989 and has remained there for all but two years.

Matt Lewis, a former columnist at the conservative Daily Caller, sums up: "I do think it's a problem, but I don't think that there is a conspiracy to bias the news," says Lewis, who recently jumped to the more mainstream Daily Beast. "But I do think that the kinds of people who go into journalism and where journalism outlets tend to be based has the inevitable outcome of slanting it not even just leftward but in a cosmopolitan, secular way."

As part of its plan for the coming years, the New York Times cites a need for more newsroom employees "from outside major metropolitan areas." Such a move might ramp up the presence of conservatives at the paper. Dean Baquet, the newspaper's executive editor, told the Erik Wemple Blog that when he <u>worked for the New Orleans Times-Picayune decades ago</u>, he had "no question in my mind that there were more conservatives" than in a big-city newsroom.

Its leadership, however, will not be asking specifically about the political orientation of recruits. "I think we absolutely do not look for a political litmus test for people in either direction," Joe Kahn, managing editor of the New York Times, told the Erik Wemple Blog in September. "The diversity challenge for us is to find a range of skills and including people who can understand and write persuasively about all aspects of American politics and society."

Likewise, The Post's Grant says, "Asking someone's political affiliations and beliefs — no, that's not part of the ordinary course of things."

CNN in 2015 launched perhaps the most ideologically targeted hiring spree in the history of journalism. As Donald Trump began rising in the polls, the 24/7 cable network realized that its existing stable of conservative commentators didn't necessarily share the views of the real estate mogul from Manhattan. So, they hired a crew of Trumpites, including, eventually, fired Trump campaign manager Corey Lewandowski. The Trump contingent had a knack for turning CNN's airwaves into logic-defying discussions, yet CNN Worldwide President Jeff Zucker defended the staffing moves. "Now, I know that there's are a lot of people who don't like Corey Lewandowski or the other Trump surrogates that we have on staff," Zucker said in October. "I think a lot of that is because they don't like the idea of the Trump candidacy and that's just a projection of 'How could you have those people on the set?' Well, we have them on the set because somebody's got to represent 14 million people who voted for the guy" in the primaries.

Like those Trump voices, young conservative journalists want to work at mainstream outlets, says Graham, if only the doors will open. "They're there for the interviewing and not just the 20-somethings," says Graham.

He cites the trajectory of journalists such as Bob Costa and Jonathan Martin, both of whom once worked for the conservative National Review and are now at The Washington Post and New York Times, respectively. But does that mean they're both conservatives?

Not necessarily, responds Graham. "Let me be blunt, though," he continues. "Any reporter who is willing to blog for the National Review without vomiting is at least somebody in whom conservatives vest hope. We are so hungry for a foothold."

A BRIEF HISTORY OF THE FILIBUSTER

The filibuster. This legislative tool, available only in the United States Senate, is defined as a parliamentary procedure to prevent a measure from being brought to a vote. The most common form of filibuster occurs when one or more senators attempt to delay or block a vote on a bill by extending debate on the measure. Politicians have used filibustering since Sen. John Calhoun created the concept in 1841. It is provided for in the Senate rules.

The notion that majority rules does not necessarily apply to the Senate; some actions require 60 votes. With its current makeup, the chances of getting 60 Senate votes to do anything meaningful, except perhaps to adjourn, is remote at best.

The filibuster is either a means of preventing bad legislation from becoming law, or of obstructing needed legislation for the public good, depending on whose ox is being gored. The rule has certain limitations and exceptions which can be altered by the Senate, but change is subject to the filibuster. The rule also provides for ending a filibuster, called cloture.

In its original form, invoking the filibuster required the senator to "take to the floor" and speak against the pending legislation; however, currently, this is no longer required. Today, senators can merely signal their intent to object, even privately, and that's enough for Senate leaders to take action. Leaders sometimes just drop the issue from floor consideration. At other times, they push ahead, taking cumbersome steps to cut off the filibuster and move forward with the proceedings.

Although its claimed purpose is to "extend debate," in practice, it's a stalling tactic. Here are five famous filibusters in U.S. history:

Jefferson Smith (James Stewart), 1939
Film's full runtime: 2 hours, 11 minutes
Sen. Jefferson Smith (played by James Stewart, the star of *Mr. Smith Goes to Washington*) filibusters a bill that will permit dam construction on the site of his proposed boys' camp; the filibuster succeeds when Sen. Harrison Paine (Claude Rains) confesses to his role in a graft scheme and tries to shoot himself.

Rand Paul, 2013
Filibuster length: 13 hours
Sen. Rand Paul, R-Ky., revived the tradition of talking filibusters, protesting U.S. drone policy by blocking a vote on CIA Director John Brennan and holding the floor for just under 13 hours. Brennan eventually won confirmation.

Huey P. Long, 1935
Filibuster length: 15 hours, 30 minutes
Sen. Huey P. Long spent 15 hours and 30 minutes arguing against passage of a New Deal bill that would have given jobs to political enemies in Louisiana. The flamboyant Long peppered his filibuster with readings of the Constitution, Shakespeare plays and oyster recipes.

Wayne Morse, 1953
Filibuster length: 22 hours, 26 minutes

Sen. Wayne Morse, an independent from Oregon, set a longevity record in filibustering over tidelands oil legislation.

Strom Thurmond, 1957
Filibuster length: 24 hours, 18 minutes

Sen. Strom Thurmond, R-S.C., broke Morse's record with an unsuccessful filibuster against the Civil Rights Act of 1957. Thurmond, subsisting on throat lozenges, malted milk tablets and a steak sandwich, spoke 24 hours and 18 minutes before concluding with the line, "I expect to vote against the bill." During his time "on the floor," Thurmond asserted that the civil rights bill was unconstitutional and constituted "cruel and unusual punishment". He went on to read documents primarily related to the United States and its history, including the Declaration of Independence, the election laws of each state in alphabetical order, a U.S. Supreme Court ruling, the U.S. Bill of Rights, and George Washington's Farewell Address. Consuming 84 pages in the Congressional Record, the filibuster cost taxpayers over $6,000 in printing costs.

In 2013, Sen. Ted Cruz, R-Texas, vowed to speak on the Senate floor "until I am no longer able to stand" in opposition to President Obama's health care law.

As can be readily seen, there is nothing that prevents a senator from reading the Manhattan telephone book, Aesop's Fables, or anything else for that matter, during his/her filibuster. A filibustering senator should wear comfortable shoes, have friendly colleagues prepared to ask questions or provide comments, and have a strong bladder. According to Senate rule, no bathroom breaks are permitted (although this can be tinkered with by careful use of one's friends).

Current debate involves either ending the filibuster completely or returning this tool to its original format of "taking the floor."

For reasons that should be self-evident, Democrats have floated the idea of complete elimination; however, at least two Democrat senators say they oppose this, causing President Biden to favor returning the filibuster to its original form. For their part, the Republicans have vowed a "scorched earth" effort to block any change.

The Democrats fear that if they make a change, it will backfire if or when the Republicans once again gain control of the Senate. Some Democrats ask whether they really believe a Republican majority won't do whatever they want regardless of what the Democrats do with their current slim majority.

So, what we have at this point is another Senate stalemate on whether to change the rule the results in a stalemate on legislation.

THE REPUBLICAN PARTY IS THE PARTY OF LINCOLN: AND SOME ACTUALLY BELIEVE IT

Recently, a Republican Party leader referred to the GOP as "The Party of Lincoln." At one time, this was true; however, this assertion overlooks our nation's history of political party realignment. Today's Republican Party is certainly NOT "The Party of Lincoln."

During debate on the 1964 Civil Rights Act, Democrat Sen. Robert Byrd of West Virginia took to the floor and filibustered this legislation for 14 hours and 13 minutes. Upon signing this act into law, President Lyndon Johnson is reported to have said "There goes the South (to the Republicans) for a generation." At that time, the south was run by Southern Democrats who very much opposed civil rights. Whether LBJ said this or not, it is prophetic, and it has lasted for generations up to the present.

(As an aside, Republican Senate Minority Leader Mitch McConnell recently said the Senate filibuster has no connection to race. He either forgets or ignores Sen Byrd's 1964 filibuster, or the 24-hour-18-minute filibuster by South Carolina Sen. Strom Thurmond in opposition to the 1957 Civil Rights Act. During his time "on the floor," Thurmond asserted that the civil rights bill was unconstitutional and constituted "cruel and unusual punishment.")

As you can see from the brief online discussion below, political party realigning is very much a part of our nation's history. Here is that history.

A **party realignment** occurs when the country transitions from being mostly run by one political party to mostly run by another political party. During party realignments, some groups of people who used to vote for one party vote for the other one. Sometimes, political parties end and new ones begin. Party realignments can happen because of important events in history or because of changes in the kinds of people in the country.

1820s

In the early 1800s, America had the "First Party System" with the Federalist Party and the Democratic-Republican Party. When James Monroe was elected President of the United States, the Federalists died out. There was an "Era of Good Feelings" of one-party rule by the Democratic-Republicans. In the United States presidential election, 1824, four different men ran for President, all as Democratic-Republicans. John Quincy Adams was elected.

After the election, Andrew Jackson formed a new party called the Democrats. Jackson's party was strongest in the South and West, and in some cities (at this time, only a few Americans lived in cities). Soon after Jackson's election, another party formed around supporters of Adams and Henry Clay. It was first called the National Republican Party, and later the Whig Party. The Whigs were strong in the North, and among the middle class and businessmen. The system of Democrats and Whigs is called the "Second Party System."

1850s-60s

After the Kansas-Nebraska Act, the "Second Party System" ended:

- Whigs and Democrats who did not want to pass the Kansas-Nebraska Act, as well as Free-Soilers, formed a new party called the Republicans. The Republicans' main goal was stopping slavery, but they also liked many of the things the Whigs liked.
- The Whig Party broke up. Some Whigs joined the Know-Nothing Party or other small parties for the 1856 election. More joined the Republicans or Democrats.
- In the 1860 election, Know-Nothings and Southern Democrats who supported the Union formed the Constitutional Union Party. During and after the American Civil War, the Know-Nothings and Unionists were part of the Republican Party.
- In 1860, what was left of the Democratic Party broke into Northern and Southern wings, one on each side of the Civil War.
- By 1868, the Democratic Party came back together and there was the "Third Party System" of Democrats and Republicans.

1930s

America went from being mostly Republican in the 1920s to mostly Democratic in the 1930s. This was due to America becoming much more urban, and the Great Depression. Franklin D. Roosevelt formed a coalition that would mostly last until 1964 called the "New Deal coalition."

- Urban areas became very Democratic. They voted very heavily for people like Al Smith and Roosevelt. They had been growing rapidly, due in part to immigrants who were part of democratic political machines.
- African American citizens had been moving from the South into large Northern cities, in large part due to racial segregation. Before the 1930s, they had either not voted or voted Republican. Under Roosevelt, they mostly voted Democratic
- Roosevelt also made gains in every part of the country, due to his mass appeal and the desire to end the depression
- For the first time in its history, the Democrats were a statist party instead of a libertarian one

1960s-80s

In the 1960s and 70s, the New Deal coalition fell apart. This was due to the Civil Rights Movement, Roe v. Wade, Vietnam War and the suburbanization of America. What changed:

- After the 1964 Civil Rights Act, many white, conservative Southern Democrats became Republicans. The South had been mostly Democratic before 1964; it was mostly Republican after (Although on the local level continued to be heavily democratic for decades).
- Many "values voters" became Republicans. These were people who voted based on morality. They thought morally good things should be legal and morally bad things should be illegal. In the 1960s, sex was closely tied to morality. In this way, people who opposed abortion and gay rights, for example Jerry Falwell, and the changes to society happening in the 1960s and 70s, became Republicans.
- Republicans also made some gains among working-class Catholics, who are mostly conservative on social issues.
- The Democrats were able to make gains among more liberal Republicans and with Latino voters.
- Working-class Democrats voted for Republicans in the 1980 election. They were called Reagan Democrats because they voted for Ronald Reagan.

So, if you come across someone representing the current Republican Party as "The Party of Lincoln," remind them about the history of political party realign

THE THREAT OF RIGHT-WING VIOLENCE

Since right-wing insurrectionists stormed the Capitol on January 6 with the vague but violent idea of taking over the government, observers are paying renewed attention to the threat of right-wing violence in our midst.

For all our focus on fighting socialism and communism, right-wing authoritarianism is actually quite an old threat in our country. The nation's focus on fighting "socialism" began in 1871, but what its opponents stood against was not government control of the means of production—an idea that never took hold in America—but the popular public policies which cost tax dollars and thus made wealthier people pay for programs that would benefit everyone. Public benefits like highways and hospitals, opponents argued, amounted to a redistribution of wealth, and thus were a leftist assault on American freedom.

In the late nineteenth and early twentieth centuries that fight against "socialism" took the form of opposition to unionization and Black rights. In the 1920s, after the Bolshevik Revolution in Russia had given shape to the American fear of socialism, making sure that system never came to America meant destroying the government regulation put in place during the Progressive Era and putting businessmen in charge of the government.

When Democrat Franklin Delano Roosevelt established business regulation, a basic social safety net, and government-funded infrastructure in the 1930s to combat the Great Depression that had laid ordinary Americans low, one right-wing senator wrote to a colleague: "This is despotism, this is tyranny, this is the annihilation of liberty.... The ordinary American is thus reduced to the status of a robot. The president has not merely signed the death warrant of capitalism, but has ordained the mutilation of the Constitution, unless the friends of liberty, regardless of party, band themselves together to regain their lost freedom."

The roots of modern right-wing extremism lie in the post-World War II reaction to FDR's New Deal and the Republican embrace of it under President Dwight D. Eisenhower. Opponents of an active government insisted that it undermined American liberty by redistributing tax dollars from hardworking white men to those eager for a handout—usually Black men, in their telling. Modern government, they insisted, was bringing socialism to America. They set out to combat it, trying to slash the government back to the form it took in the 1920s.

Their job got easier after 1987, when the Fairness Doctrine ended. That Federal Communications Commission policy had required public media channels to base their stories on fact and to present both sides of a question. When it was gone, talk radio took off, hosted by radio jocks like Rush Limbaugh who contrasted their ideal country with what they saw as the socialism around them: a world in which hardworking white men who took care of their wives and children were hemmed in by government that was taxing them to give benefits to lazy people of color and "Feminazis." These "Liberals" were undermining the country and the family, aided and abetted by lawmakers building a big government that sucked tax dollars.

In August 1992, the idea that hardworking white men trying to take care of their families were endangered by an intrusive government took shape at Ruby Ridge, Idaho. Randy Weaver, a former factory worker who had moved his family to northern Idaho to escape what he saw as the corruption of American society, failed to show up for trial on a firearms charge. When federal marshals tried to arrest him, a firefight left Weaver's fourteen-year-old son and a deputy marshal dead. In the aftermath of the shooting, federal and local officers laid an 11-day siege to the Weavers' cabin, and a sniper wounded Weaver and killed his wife, Vicki.

Right-wing activists and neo-Nazis from a nearby Aryan Nations compound swarmed to Ruby Ridge to protest the government's attack on what they saw as a man protecting his family. Negotiators eventually brought Weaver out, but the standoff at Ruby Ridge convinced western men they had to arm themselves to fight off the government.

In February of the next year, during the Democratic Bill Clinton administration, the same theme played out in Waco, Texas, when officers stormed the compound of a religious cult whose former members reported that their leader, David Koresh, was stockpiling weapons. A gun battle and a fire ended the 51-day siege on April 19, 1993. Seventy-six people died.

While a Republican investigation cited "overwhelming evidence" that exonerated the government of wrongdoing, talk radio hosts nonetheless railed against the Democratic administration, especially Attorney General Janet Reno, for the events at Waco. What happened there fit neatly into what was by then the Republican narrative of an overreaching government that crushed individuals, and political figures harped on that idea.

Rush Limbaugh stoked his listeners' anger with reports of the "Waco invasion" and talked of the government's "murder" of citizens, making much of the idea that a group of Christians had been killed by a female government official who was single and— as opponents made much of— unfeminine (reactionary rocker Ted Nugent featured an obscene caricature of her for years in his stage version of "Kiss My Glock").

Horrified by the government's attempt to break into the cult's compound, Alex Jones, who would go on to become an important conspiracy theorist and founder of InfoWars, dropped out of community college to start a talk show on which he warned that Reno had "murdered" the people at Waco and that the government was about to impose martial law. The modern militia movement took off.

The combination of political rhetoric and violence radicalized a former Army gunner, Timothy McVeigh, who decided to bring the war home to the government. "Taxes are a joke," he wrote to a newspaper in 1992. "More taxes are always the answer to government mismanagement…. Is a Civil War Imminent? Do we have to shed blood to reform the current system? I hope it doesn't come to that. But it might."

On April 19, 1995, a date chosen to honor the Waco standoff, McVeigh set off a bomb at the Alfred P. Murrah Federal Building in Oklahoma City. The blast killed 168 people, including 19 children younger than six, and wounded more than 800. When the police captured McVeigh, he was wearing a T-shirt with a picture of Abraham Lincoln and the words "Sic Semper Tyrannis." The same words John Wilkes Booth shouted after he assassinated Lincoln, they mean "thus always to tyrants," and are the words attributed to Brutus after he and his supporters murdered Caesar.

By 1995, right-wing terrorists envisioned themselves as protectors of American individualism in the face of a socialist government, but the reality was that their complaints were not about government activism. They were about who benefited from that activism.

In 2014, Nevada cattle rancher Cliven Bundy brought the contradictions in this individualist image to light when he fought the government over the impoundment of the cattle that he had been grazing on public land for more than 20 president, seeking to overturn the election based on nothing more than allegations of fraud and election rigging rejected by every judge—liberal and conservative--who presided over more than 60 cases in several states, including two unanimously rejected by the United States Supreme Court.

The effect of such an effort is to reject the will of the people by overturning a valid election, and install the losing candidate/incumbent as president. This amounts to an attempted coup rejecting constitutional norms and the principles governing our form of government.

Each member of Congress took an oath to "solemnly swear (or affirm) that I will support and defend the Constitution of the United States against all enemies, foreign and domestic; that I will bear true faith and allegiance to the same; that I take this obligation freely, without any mental reservation or purpose of evasion…."

The definition of treason includes an attempt to overthrow the government. The actions of these House members is an attempt to overthrow the government as elected by the people and Electoral College, and install an incumbent who lost the election and the Electoral College vote.

Whatever may be the result, one thing is clear. For their efforts to reject the results of a free and fair election, the votes of the Electoral College, and disregard the unanimous Supreme Court decisions and court decisions in more than 60 cases, these House members have violated their oath of office and should be censured or expelled from Congress.

And the several Attorneys General who signed on to Texas' frivolous lawsuit in the Supreme Court should face appropriate discipline by their respective state bar associations.

One's conduct has consequences. One is certainly free to act; however, one must act responsibly, and be held accountable when those actions do violence to the constitution and laws. Such is the case here.

These elected officials made their bed; now they should be required to sleep in it.

PRESIDENTIAL LEADERSHIP AND OTHER QUOTES

On Mindset

"Nothing can stop the man with the right mental attitude from achieving his goal; nothing on earth can help the man with the wrong mental attitude." ~Thomas Jefferson

"If you see ten troubles coming down the road, you can be sure that nine will run into the ditch before they reach you." ~Calvin Coolidge

"Men are not prisoners of fate, but only prisoners of their own minds." ~Franklin D. Roosevelt

"Pessimism never won any battle." ~Dwight D. Eisenhower

of free speech. It embraces freedom of the press. Hugo Black

3. The Founding Fathers gave the free press the protection it must have to bear the secrets of government and inform the people. Hugo Black

4. Without a free press there can be no free society. That is axiomatic. However, freedom of the press is not an end in itself but a means to the end of a free society. The scope and nature of the constitutional guarantee of the freedom of the press are to be viewed and applied in that light. Felix Frankfurter

5. The very purpose of a Bill of Rights was to withdraw certain subjects from the vicissitudes of political controversy. One's right to life, liberty and property, to free speech, a free press, freedom of worship and assembly may not be submitted to vote; they depend on no elections. Robert H. Jackson

Journalist & Reporters

1. Freedom of the press is not just important to democracy, it is democracy. Walter Cronkite

2. Freedom of the press, or, to be more precise, the benefit of freedom of the press, belongs to everyone – to the citizen as well as the publisher… The crux is not the publisher's 'freedom to print'; it is, rather, the citizen's 'right to know.' – Arthur Hays Sulzberge

3. As someone who is in awe and grateful every day to be in a country where freedom of the press, free speech and free elections are a way of life, I am

wowed, amazed and excited by the opportunity to moderate a 2012 presidential debate. Candy Crowley

4. If the true freedom of the press is to decide for itself what to publish and when to publish it, the true responsibility of the press must be to assert and defend that freedom... What the press in America needs is less inhibition, not more restraint. Tom Wicker

5. The freedom of the press is one of the great bulwarks of liberty, and can never be restrained but by despotic governments. George Mason

6. I think the important thing is that there be plenty of newspapers, with plenty of different people controlling them, so that there are a variety of viewpoints, so there is a choice for the public. This is the freedom of the press that is needed. Rupert Murdoch

Famous Writers and their statements that make you think

1. I avow that I do not hold that complete and instantaneous love for the freedom of the press that one accords to things whose nature is unqualifiedly good. I love it out of consideration for the evils it prevents much more than for the good it does. Alexis de Tocqueville

2. The freedom of speech and the freedom of the press have not been granted to the people in order that they may say things which please, and which are based upon accepted thought, but the right to say the things

which displease, the right to say the things which convey the new and yet unexpected thoughts, the right to say things, even though they do a wrong. Samuel Gompers

3. Whenever there is injustice, there is tension. But in China it is very hard to release your anger unless you burn yourself or you jump from a bridge. In a society where there is no freedom of the press, it is difficult for victims to be noticed. Ai Weiwei

4. I recognize the need to provide the press – and, through you, the American people – with information to the fullest extent possible. In our democracy, the work of the Pentagon press corps is important, defending our freedom and way of life is what this conflict is about, and that certainly includes freedom of the press. – Donald Rumsfeld

5. After visits to several Communist countries (USSR, Poland, Czechoslovakia, Slovenia, East Germany, Vietnam, China, Cuba), I feel strongly that most "revolutionary" types around the world don't realize the importance of freedom of the press and the air, a right to peaceably assemble and discuss anything, including the dangers of such discussions. Pete Seeger

6. Freedom of the press is the mortar that binds together the bricks of democracy — and it is also the open window embedded in those bricks. Shashi Tharoor

7. I'm not a big fan of regulation: anyone who likes freedom of the press can't be. Julian Assange

8. Freedom of the Press, if it means anything at all, means the freedom to criticize and oppose George Orwell

9. At any given moment there is an orthodoxy, a body of ideas of which it is assumed that all right-thinking people will accept without question. It is not exactly forbidden to say this, that or the other, but it is "not done" to say it… Anyone who challenges the prevailing orthodoxy finds himself silenced with surprising effectiveness. A genuinely unfashionable opinion is almost never given a fair hearing, either in the popular press or in the high-brow periodicals. – George Orwell

10. The liberty of the press is a blessing when we are inclined to write against others, and a calamity when we find ourselves overborne by the multitude of our assailants. Samuel Johnson

11. One of the unsung freedoms that go with a free press is the freedom not to read it. Ferdinand Mount

12. Without general elections, without freedom of the press, freedom of speech, freedom of assembly, without the free battle of opinions, life in every public institution withers away, becomes a caricature of itself, and bureaucracy rises as the only deciding factor. Rosa Luxemburg

13. Woe to that nation whose literature is cut short by the intrusion of force. This is not merely interference with freedom of the press but the sealing up of a nation's heart, the excision of its memory. Aleksandr Solzhenitsyn

14. To struggle against censorship, whatever its nature, and whatever the power under which it exists, is my duty as a writer, as are calls for freedom of the press. I am a passionate supporter of that freedom, and I consider that if any writer were to imagine that he could prove he didn't need that freedom, then he would be like a fish affirming in public that it didn't need water. Mikhail Bulgakov

15. Freedom of speech, freedom of the press, and freedom of religion all have a double aspect – freedom of thought and freedom of action. Frank Murphy

16. Without freedom of the press, there can be no representative government. Charles Maurice de Talleyrand

17. Freedom of the press is to the machinery of the state what the safety valve is to the steam engine. Arthur Schopenhauer

18. We don't have an Official Secrets Act in the United States, as other countries do. Under the First Amendment, freedom of the press, freedom of speech, and freedom of association are more important than protecting secrets. Alan Dershowitz

19. Criticism

20. Freedom of the press is essential to the preservation of a democracy; but there is a difference between freedom and license. Editorialists who tell downright lies in order to advance their own agendas do more to discredit the press than all the censors in the world. Franklin D. Roosevelt

21. If you think there is freedom of the press in the United States, I tell you there is no freedom of the press… They come out with the cheap shot. The press should be ashamed of itself. They should come to both sides of the issue and hear both sides and let the American people make up their minds. Bill Moyers

22. From the essay "Twenty-five Things People Have a Shocking Capacity to Be Surprised by Over and Over Again" 1. Journalists sometimes make things up. 2. Journalists sometimes get things wrong. 3. Almost all books that are published as memoirs were initially written as novels, and then the agent/editor said, this might work better as a memoir. 6. Freedom of the press belongs to the man who owns one. Nora Ephron

23. When one makes a Revolution, one cannot mark time; one must always go forward – or go back. He who now talks about the 'freedom of the press' goes backward, and halts our headlong course towards Socialism. Vladimir Lenin

24. In Czechoslovakia there is no such thing as freedom of the press. In the United States there is no such thing as freedom from the press. Martina Navratilova

25. The bourgeoisie is many times stronger than we. To give it the weapon of freedom of the press is to ease the enemy's cause, to help the class enemy. We do not desire to end in suicide, so we will not do this. Vladimir Lenin

26. Why should freedom of speech and freedom of press be allowed? Why should a government which is doing what it believes to be right allow itself to be criticized? It would not allow opposition by lethal weapons. Ideas are much more fatal things than guns. Why should any man be allowed to buy a printing press and disseminate pernicious opinions calculated to embarrass the government? Vladimir Lenin

27. Those who write the editorials and those who write the columns, they simply are unaccountable. They're free to impose their cultural politics in the name of freedom of the press. Jesse Jackson

28. Every time I criticize what I consider to be excesses or faults in the news business, I am accused of repression, and the leaders of various media professional groups wave the First Amendment as they denounce me. That happens to be my amendment, too. It guarantees my free speech as it does their freedom of the press... There is room for all of us – and for our divergent views – under the First Amendment. – Spiro T. Agnew

29. Freedom of the press, freedom of the news media, must be subordinated to the overriding needs of the integrity of Singapore, and to the primacy of purpose of an elected government. – Lee Kuan Yew

30. We must do away with all newspapers. A revolution cannot be accomplished with freedom of the press. Che Guevara

31. Freedom of press and freedom of speech: What a blessing for a country while in the hands of honest,

patriotic men; what a curse if in the hands of designing demagogues. William J. H. Boetcker

32. To get the inestimable good that freedom of the press assures one must know how to submit to the inevitable evil it gives rise to. Alexis de Tocqueville

33. What have the Germans gained by their boasted freedom of the press, except the liberty of abusing each other as they like? Johann Wolfgang von Goethe

34. It is almost superfluous to say that there is no such thing as a free and independent press among the mainstream news media today. In fact, the major media more resembles a propaganda machine than it does a free press. Chuck Baldwin

35. We have more freedom of the press than any other country in a similar position. Even way back in the frightened '50s, Communists, for example, could publish their magazine. The KKK published their own books. But face it, the mass media is controlled by money. Pete Seeger

36. There is an urgent need to-day for the citizens of a democracy to think well. It is not enough to have freedom of the Press and parliamentary institutions. Our difficulties are due partly to our own stupidity, partly to the exploitation of that stupidity, and partly to our own prejudices and personal desires. Susan Stebbing

37. Some of the press who speak loudly about the freedom of the press are themselves the enemies of freedom. Countless people dare not say a thing because they know it will be picked up and made a

song of by the press. That limits freedom. Geoffrey Fisher

38. Freedom of the press belongs to the man who owns one. A. J. Liebling

39. The full impact of printing did not become possible until the adoption of the Bill of Rights in the United States with its guarantee of freedom of the press. A guarantee of freedom of the press in print was intended to further sanctify the printed word and to provide a rigid bulwark for the shelter of vested interests. Harold Innis

40. Much as constitutional guarantees of press freedom do little good for prospective publishers if they do not have access to paper or ink, the right to aid in dying is strikingly useless if nobody is willing to help. Jacob M. Appel

41. Never get into a fight with someone who buys ink by the barrel.

42. Free inquiry entails recognition of civil liberties as integral to its pursuit, that is, a free press, freedom of communication, the right to organize opposition parties and to join voluntary associations, and freedom to cultivate and publish the fruits of scientific, philosophical, artistic, literary, moral and religious freedom. Paul Kurtz

43. How can you have in our country that is based upon liberality and liberation, be so anti-liberal. That's toxic waste to our consciousness. It's hard to be an American conservative because that's a contradiction in terms. Now if you take away freedom of speech,

freedom of press, freedom of protest, and lock people out based upon their race, their language and their religion, that's conservative and fascist. America is a liberal idea. Jesse Jackson

44. Freedom of the press is a precious privilege that no country can forego. Mahatma Gandhi

45. All Americans value the freedom of speech and the freedom of the press, and I believe this is essential for our continued way of life. But with this freedom comes responsibility. That responsibility has been abdicated here by some in the media and some in the government. Steven Hatfill

46. Town after town has but one newspaper or one radio station. It is often owned by Murdoch. Yes, we don't have as much freedom of the press as we think we have – although the traditional freedom of speech is strongly rooted in American culture. Pete Seeger

47. As people get their opinions so largely from the newspapers they read, the corruption of the schools would not matter so much if the Press were free. But the Press is not free. As it costs at least a quarter of a million of money to establish a daily newspaper in London, the newspapers are owned by rich men. And they depend on the advertisements of other rich men. Editors and journalists who express opinions in print that are opposed to the interests of the rich are dismissed and replaced by subservient ones. George Bernard Shaw

48. Socialism is a scare word they have hurled at every advance the people have made in the last 20 years.

49. Socialism is what they called public power.
50. Socialism is what they called social security.
51. Socialism is what they called farm price supports.
52. Socialism is what they called bank deposit insurance.
53. Socialism is what they called the growth of free and independent labor organizations.
54. Socialism is their name for almost anything that helps all the people.

Harry Truman 1952

WHAT IS FASCISM?

Fascism a political philosophy, movement, or regime (such as that of the Fascisti) that exalts nation and often race above the individual and that stands for a centralized autocratic government headed by a dictatorial leader, severe economic and social regimentation, and forcible suppression of opposition. Fascists believe that liberal democracy is obsolete and regard the complete mobilization of society under a totalitarian one-party state as necessary to prepare a nation for armed conflict and to respond effectively to economic difficulties. A fascist state is led by a strong leader such as a dictator and a martial law government composed of the members of the governing fascist party to forge national unity and maintain a stable and orderly society.

Fascism rejects assertions that violence is automatically negative in nature and views imperialism, political violence and war as means that can achieve national rejuvenation. Fascists advocate a mixed economy, with the principal goal of achieving autarky (national economic self-sufficiency) through protectionist and economic interventionist policies.] The extreme authoritarianism and nationalism of fascism often manifests a belief in racial "purity" or a "master race", usually synthesized with some variant of racism or bigotry of a demonized other; the idea of "purity" has motivated fascist regimes to commit massacres, forced sterilizations, genocides, mass killings or forced deportations against a perceived other.

HOW TO COPE WITH A PANDEMIC

Those of us in our senior years can reflect on how we're handling ourselves during the pandemic through what you write. For me, I find it best that trying to keep my daily routine as close to normal as possible. Harriet and I go to the gym and walk two miles every other day. I will start going back to the pool on the days I don't walk. We go out for dinner three times a week, once by ourselves and twice with friends. We do our shopping once a week. Of course, we choose restaurants that are familiar to us; make sure the staff is masked; and we wear masks until we're seated. And we go early when the restaurants are not too crowded.

We are fully vaccinated, and will get our booster shot when our doctor calls us, as she did when the two shots became available earlier this year. Wearing a mask is such a minor, insignificant thing when you consider the risks. I only wish more people would put the public health and well-being above their false sense of personal rights. We are a nation of laws that impose responsibilities on us for our conduct. There is no right without a concomitant responsibility. People can't decide for themselves whether to stop at a red light or stop sign. There are consequences for failing to do so. Don't want to wear a seatbelt?

If you're stopped, you will wish you had. Want to own a car? Better have insurance and a valid license. Want to be a doctor, lawyer, engineer, construction worker, etc.? Better have the education, earn the necessary credentials, pass the necessary tests and get the necessary license. You get the point. Our lives are regulated every day, yet we accept this because this is how we function in a Democracy of 340 million people.

THE SUPREME COURT'S DARK HISTORY

The Supreme Court has a history of not addressing the needs of the people. Plessy v. Ferguson is a primary example. Other decisions upholding Jim Crow laws, as well as rejecting FDR's efforts to deal with the Great Depression, also show the Court at its lowest ebb. Of course, eventually, Plessy was rejected, as were those efforts to curtail FDR's programs in the 1930s, but the fact is people were hurt by Supreme Court decisions.

We are going through another cycle now, with the Supreme Court focusing more on businesses and corporate well-being than ordinary people. Think Citizens United. But the majority Republican Court, in this instance, is clever enough to kick the can to Congress, where getting little or nothing done is the current fare. Congress, of course, won't step in to help those about to be evicted. I also had the privilege of arguing before the Court. Back when Brennan, Marshall and Stevens were on the Court. It's a far cry from what we have today. History is cyclical; we will get through this cycle. Our better angels, in Abraham Lincoln's words, will prevail.

THE WOES OF THE MASONS

The Masonic Association of North America, up through 2017, annually published a list of the number of Masons in all the states and provinces. As the numbers for the United States went from more than 4 million in 1959 to just under 1.1 million in 2017, they stopped the annual publication....until recently when they published the numbers for 2018-2020.

During this three-year period, we lost over 125,000 Masons. We now have less than 900,000 Masons in the United States. This is the lowest number ever recorded in more than 100 years of the organization's existence. I recall a past grand master telling me that he envisioned a fraternity of 200 lodges and 20,000 members. It appears he was most prophetic.

What is significant is that the number of annual losses remains high, even as the total number of Masons drops. This means we're losing members from a smaller and smaller pool. My overriding concern is sustainability. As the numbers shrink, either dues will have to go up significantly to support our fraternity, or services will have to be cut back. Or both.

There was talk a few years ago about how Masonry is going to turn around these numbers. These numbers from the association belie that. I think Masonry will survive, but along the line of what this past grand master said. We will focus purely on the lodge, with little (if any) community outreach like the Masons had during the glory years of 3-4 million members, simply because the numbers of the past, and the influence those numbers brought to their communities, won't be there in the future.

WHAT IF THE CONSTITUTION WERE CHANGED?

Here's the real danger point. We can certainly wax on about unconstitutional legislation, but what if the Constitution were changed? After all, it's the interpretation of its language that gives it life. According to the Congressional Research Service, the US Supreme Court has reversed itself on constitutional precedent more than 140 times.

What is to prevent that Court, and the lower federal courts and even state supreme courts, to say that what was constitutional isn't anymore? We know there are attacks on Roe v. Wade, First Amendment libel principles, expansion of the Second Amendment, church and state separation, subjects taught in schools, etc.

What is to prevent the judiciary from buying into the doctrinal demands of the far right? What is to prevent the judiciary from declaring that the Warren Court had it all wrong? In Texas, we have neighbors legally authorized to snoop on neighbors regarding abortion, but suppose this were extended to simply voicing "unpopular" opinions? Can disagreements become the cause for arrest and punishment? I pose these questions because once a path is taken, it can easily and quickly become a slippery slope.

THE SUPREME COURT'S HISTORY OF OVERRULING ITSELF ON CONSTITUTIONAL ISSUES

I just finished reading United States Supreme Court Justice Stephen Breyer's latest book "The Authority of the Court and the Peril of Politics." It's an essay of less than 50 pages of actual text, in which Justice Breyer echoes his colleague Amy Coney Barrett's view that the Court is not made up of politically partisan hacks.

Justice Breyer asks the reader not to confuse philosophical difference with political motivation. Judges are not politicians, he says. Justices (and judges) apply a host of interpretive tools in order to reach what they consider to be "the rule of law." We can all agree that adherence to the rule of law is essential to our Democracy. But what exactly is the rule of law?

In 2018, the Congressional Research Service published a report entitled "The Supreme Court's Overruling of Constitutional Precedent." That report reveals that the Court has overruled itself on matters of constitutional law 141 times!

Plessy v. Ferguson, an 1896 case, upheld the constitutionality of racial segregation. Did this case represent the rule of law? In 1954, Brown v. Board of Education rejected racial segregation. What happened to the Plessy rule of law?

In 1944, Korematsu v. United States, the Court held that compelling exclusion (and confinement) of citizens during time of war was justified to reduce the risk of espionage. Again, was this the rule of law? This case was rejected in Trump v. Hawaii last year.

The answer to these questions is all decisions of the Supreme Court that attained a majority vote were and are the rule of law at the time.

What caused these changes to the rule of law? What caused the Court to reject precedent in favor of a new rule of law? The answer should be obvious: a change in the composition of the Court itself.

Members of the judiciary, and other commentators as well, point out how decisions are reached. They wax about the importance of precedent, history, plain meaning or contemporaneous construction of constitutional provisions; with a statute, they consider ordinary meaning, statutory context, canons of construction, legislative history, and evidence of the way a statute was enacted.

Justices Breyer and Barrett are properly concerned that more and more people are losing confidence in the judiciary, particularly on hot-button social issues in which they view the Court out of touch with contemporaneous times. They ask that the public understand how judicial decisions— particularly those at the highest level—are arrived at, and that whether they agree or disagree with a decision, they accept the rulings and move on.

But in times of great division, this becomes more and more difficult. There are those who with great skepticism view the rule of law as whatever five justices say it is, or whatever those in power want it to be, like outlawing riots without defining what it is, thereby implicating or chilling constitutionally protected peaceful protests. Or justifying recently adopted voter suppression laws upon a non-existent claim of voter fraud. Or opposing vaccinations and the wearing of masks in the name of freedom and liberty in the face of a national as well as worldwide pandemic, while denying women of their liberty and freedom to decide their own health issues pertaining to abortion.

Words are fine; they matter. But actions do speak louder than words. Our judiciary is ultimately judged by how the courts deal with social issues; issues that matter directly to the vast majority of the populace. And that is how the public will eventually react to both Breyer's and Barrett's plea.

WHY IS THE STUDY OF HISTORY SO IMPORTANT?

Recently, I had a lengthy discussion with a staunchly conservative colleague on the subject of progressive legislation and the New Deal. He vehemently maintained that the New Deal did not end the Great Depression; only the rapid mobilization to fight World War II did.

While I agreed in part that the war certainly ended the years of social misery following the 1929 stock market crash, the New Deal certainly paved the road toward ending the Depression.

My colleague disagreed with me.

To me, this discussion tells me why knowledge of history is so important, including its context. As you will shortly see, my colleague's view is flat-out historically wrong, and it represents an either-or view of history without the nuances and context that history's lessons must consider.

You can go onto any search engine and find the numerous laws proposed by the FDR administration and enacted by the New Deal Congress from 1933 to 1939.

In 1935 and 1936, the Supreme Court declared unconstitutional laws securing a minimum wage, maximum work hours, and the right to unionize for workers. It rejected pension programs and child labor restrictions, price codes and farm subsidies. These cases include the Railroad Retirement Act, the Bituminous Coal Conservation Act, and, more importantly for more expansive coverage, the Agricultural Adjustment Act and the National Industrial Recovery Act.

The court's decisions in invalidating these measures generally maintained the long tradition of laissez-faire economics. The majorities supporting these decisions based them on a conservative reading of the Constitution. This included a strict reading of the Tenth Amendment that says powers not granted to the federal government in the Constitution are reserved for the states or the people. "The Constitution grants to Congress no power to regulate for the promotion of the general welfare," as the majority proclaimed in a 1936 case striking down a minimum wage and other regulation in the coal industry.

The court also referred to the due process clauses of the Fifth and Fourteenth Amendments, finding that laws governing workplace issues infringed on the liberty of individuals to enter contracts under whatever terms they chose. And the court narrowly interpreted the federal government's authority under the Constitution to regulate interstate commerce, shielding places of production— from mines to chicken plants—from federal oversight.

These rulings ultimately led Roosevelt to conceive of a court-packing plan. Although this plan attracted much opposition, the court itself began upholding New Deal legislation. This ended any effort toward a court-packing scheme.

As I mentioned earlier, context is important. A central question is what New Deal legislation was in effect at the start of World War II. Social Security became law in 1935. Wages and hours legislation took effect in 1938, and certain pension plans were in effect.

The chart below shows that the percentage of unemployed dropped during the period leading up to the war:

Year				
1931	15.9%	-6.4%	-9.3%	Dust Bowl
1932	23.6%	-12.9%	-10.3%	Hoover's tax hikes
1933	24.9%	-1.2%	0.8%	FDR's New Deal
1934	21.7%	10.8%	1.5%	Depression eased thanks to New Deal
1935	20.1%	8.9%	3.0%	
1936	16.9%	12.9%	1.4%	
1937	14.3%	5.1%	2.9%	Spending cuts
1938	19.0%	-3.3%	-2.8%	FLSA starts min wage
1939	17.2%	8.0%	0%	Drought ended
1940	14.6%			

In looking at this chart, remember that in 1935 and 1936, the court declared critical programs unconstitutional. Congress thus had to re-enact legislation that the court ultimately validate. This, at least in part, explains the percentages of unemployed.

So, back to the original question. Did the New Deal end the Great Depression, or did World War II end it? The answer is the war hastened the end of the depression, but the New Deal certainly paved the way.

WE ARE LIVING THROUGH 1984 AND NEWSPEAK

Comments posted by others point out the most serious threat to our more than 200-year-old experiment with representative Democracy. I recall when Nikita Khrushchev said "we will bury you" in the 1950s. He wasn't referring to a military victory; he was referring to internal collapse. When those who commit treasonous acts are called "patriots;" when those who defend our form of government, and its most visible symbol in Washington, D.C., are deemed "the enemy;" when elected officials engage in denial and stoke the flames by arousing the gullible and misled with mindless bellicose rants and lies; we have an existential crisis at home.

Those who represent "our better angels" must come forth and vigorously call out the ringleaders and cultists before a vocal minority undermines our form of government and way of life. Those Republicans who are appalled at what has happened to their party must unite with Democrats, Independents and others and in one voice condemn those who, in the name of freedom, liberty and Democracy, seek to undermine them--or worse. Once again, those oft-repeated words ring true: Those who fail to learn the lessons of history are condemned to repeat them.

The concern for a dystopian future is far more real than imagined, and it's closer than we might think. We know the current iteration of the Republican Party, fresh off of its voter suppression efforts built on the voter fraud lie, will use the upcoming reapportionment and redistricting processes to gerrymander House and state legislative districts take over the House and more state legislatures.

Look how close they came in 2020. If that happens, and the Senate falls into the Republican Party's hands, only Biden's veto power will stand between what we had the four years prior to this past January--and it might even be worse, with more violence. And if a smoother, more polished candidate, but nevertheless beholden to Trump and his base, manages to win in 2024, this will give the Republicans more time to further re-shape the judiciary, making recent self-serving claims by some of the Supreme Court Justices that political partisanship plays no role in the high court ring hollow.

And you can be certain that, by following the party's history, efforts will be made to curtain social programs, provide more benefits to the wealthy, undermine relationships with allies, etc. Just look at how the Republican Party functioned following WW I, leading up to the 1929 crash, leading up to WW II, etc. History does repeat itself. This appears to be the Republican game plan. If by "the cannons," you mean having the real Republicans join forces with Democrats, Independents and others and in no uncertain terms call out the loonies, crazies and wild-eyed for what they really are, then this must be done sooner rather than later, or by 2025, the die will have been cast.

Although a presidential election gauges national voter sentiment, look at how many presidents in recent times were elected not by popular vote, but by the Electoral College. We can readily see what the results of the confluence of voter suppression legislation and partisan gerrymandering will be. This is not the time for those who see what is happening to make their voices heard.

I just finished "Peril" by Bob Woodward and Robert Costa. What stands out is how close we came to a fait accompli insurrection. If it hadn't been for a few "better angels" in of the Trump Administration--and a few Republican members of Congress who, albeit timidly, stood up to him and his repeated lies about the election--the outcome of January 6 might have been drastically different. Notice that no one on the right is coming forth claiming the bombshells in the book are "fake news" or flat-out lies.

No one has threatened libel actions. In fact, the book has been largely greeted by silence on the right. But also absent is any sense of righteous outrage or moral indignation by the moderates and the left. The attitude seems to be "ho hum, another book about Trumpism."

This six-point plan to have the vice president overturn the election is the most shocking point in the book (but by no means the only one); regardless of its outlandishness, it remains a blueprint for potential future use. At bottom, this book is not so much about the past, as it is a warning for the future. The authors remind us that Trump is still out there; and even after January 6, Trumpism is still alive and supported by a base of tens of millions. Trump's most ardent supporters, including lawyers, might be branded as crazies or loonies, but it would be a mistake to simply dismiss them. The last sentence of the book is most telling: "Peril remains."

THIS IS FOR THOSE WHO VALUE A FREE PRESS AND THE PUBLIC'S RIGHT TO KNOW; A PERSONAL STORY

More than two weeks have now passed since the tragic death of a friend and colleague, and still there has been no news report on the details of the vehicle accident, due to a Florida law known as Marsy's Law. This law is supposed to protect against the disclosure of the identity of crime victims; what it does is adversely impact the ability to report the news and inform the public.

When I was in journalism school at the University of Florida, I was drilled in getting the who, what, when, where, why and how of a situation in order to fully report the story. I wonder if this is still taught today.

I knew Chesterfield "Chet" Smith, Jr. I worked with him in the Attorney General's Office for more than 16 years. His tragic death was a major news story, as demonstrated by its recent front-page treatment in the <u>Democrat</u>. Sadly, however, what was missing from that article is the who, what, where, why and how of the story. Briefly put, who was the driver? Was the driver impaired, distracted, etc.? What was the placement of the vehicle and Chet's bicycle at the time of the collision?

What actually happened that led to his death? How and why did the accident happen? Was a crime committed by the driver? If so, have charges been filed? I could go on and on.

And this is by no means the only time information of this nature has been hidden from the public under this law. Another vehicular accident was reported as awaiting further information in the form of a press release.

This naturally leads to the bigger question: what other information of public interest goes unreported either because government hasn't disclosed, or the press hasn't been aggressive enough in seeking answers and accountability?

I know Marsy's Law is designed to protect the victim. In fact, it was the media lawyers who interpreted this law to apply in this particular incident. But who is the victim here? Certainly Chet is; and now, as a result of the article, that is public knowledge. But what about driver? Is she a victim, too, and if so, of what? And even if she somehow fits that definition, we still don't know what happened. How would a description of what, where, why and how the accident happened implicate the driver's privacy, assuming she is considered a victim?

Law enforcement evidently maintains that the investigation is ongoing. One of the things I learned in journalism school is to read between the lines. Such a reading of the skeletal news accounts thus far makes me skeptical of the reason for the silence. It doesn't take very long to determine whether a driver is impaired. Alcohol on the breath. Inability to walk a straight line. What she distracted? A cell phone in the car could certainly point this out, as could the answers to a few basic questions. And there is still the matter of how and why this accident happened, without implicating privacy. My instincts tell me there is more to this story.

When this type of situation occurs, it inevitably leads to speculation and, worse, rumors. One that came to me is whether the driver is, or is related to, a prominent person in the community. Without the full story, this type of rumor can spread fast. It may well be that the media are waiting for law enforcement to make a statement. If so, then certainly this fact should be reported. It may well be that law enforcement believes that Marsy's law allows them to keep this information from the public indefinitely. If so, this, too, should be reported. And this latter possibility graphically demonstrates the draconian impact of this law on news gathering, dissemination and an informed public.

The media's ability to be faithful to the First Amendment, and the public's right to know, take a beating if and when they must depend on a press release from government. (Assuming that this law would survive a challenge under the First Amendment should the media choose to publish this information. Recall the Pentagon Papers story of 50 year ago.) It must never be up to the government to decide what is and what is not to be reported as news. Laws such as Marsy's Law can have the effect of intimidating the media, leading them to shy away from reporting newsworthy events. The media must never become so timid that it either interprets a law that undermines their constitutional grant of a free and independent press as one of the great bulwarks of liberty, or shies away from their primary role as guardians of our Democracy.

Recall these words from Donald Rumsfeld: "You don't know what you don't know." And if we don't know something, how can we make informed judgments, upon which Democracy depends? This from the Washington Post: "Democracy dies in darkness."

WHY DOES TRUMP SAY WHAT HE SAYS AND DOES WHAT HE DOES?

Trump will continue to say what he's been saying, and act as he's been acting, because it worked in 2016; almost worked in 2020; and he believes it will work in 2022 and 2024. The scary part is he may be right. Democrats, Independents and disgruntled traditional Republicans wanted Trump gone, and believed that quick and decisive action by the Biden Administration--bolstered by a slim majority in Congress--would neutralize Trump-- and, more importantly, Trumpism--for the future.

However, instead of positive action directed at long neglected problems, we have a Democratic Party seemingly at war with itself. Progressive and moderates are at loggerheads over how to craft policies on infrastructure, immigration, climate change, etc. And what happens where there is no solid, positive leadership, especially where it's expected quickly? A vacuum occurs. And it is precisely that vacuum that Trump and Trumpism hope to fill by taking both houses of Congress in 2022, and the White House two years later.

Those who expected Biden to show strong leadership from the get-go have been witnesses to the boondoggle of the Afghanistan withdrawal, and stalemate over the budget, infrastructure, immigration, social programs, etc. As Biden evidently tries to use quiet diplomacy to get the progressives and moderates in his own party on board, he also evidently thinks he's dealing with the traditional Republican Party rather than the one taken over by Trump. The congressional Republicans are using delaying tactics, stalling for time until the 2022 midterm cycle kicks off.

Biden's window of opportunity remains open, but it's rapidly closing; he doesn't have the luxury of another full year to show decisive leadership while reminding of the four previous years. Trump is banking on a frustrated and angry electorate as he did in 2016. The Biden Administration must show strength of leadership and legislative success in key areas over the next few months. Voters in 2022 and 2024 won't remember his only major legislative success thus far; we know people have short memory spans when it comes to elections. These hot-button issues must be met with legislation truly designed to fix problems. If that fails.....

WHAT ARE WE ENTITLED TO KNOW?

How much do we really know? This is for the lawyers out there, and for those who value an informed citizenry.

Current efforts to prevent the teaching of critical race theory and former President Trump's attempt to prevent Congress from gaining access to records pertaining to the January 6 attack on our Capitol (among other things) raise an important question: Does the public have a constitutional right to know? The only Supreme Court cases that I have found that address this right is in the context of the Freedom of Information Act. But is the right to know based on whether Congress (or a state legislature) decides to enact a law that gives the public this right? If the answer is yes, then any right so granted can be amended or repealed. In short, the public's right to know is therefore up to the legislative branch of government.

One commentator said "The Constitution may be readily understood to grant a public right to know certain types of information. Specifically, the Constitution imposes an obligation on the government to publish two categories of information: a Journal of Congress (Article I, section 5) and a statement and account of all receipts and expenditures (Article I, section 9). And the government's obligation to publish this information is semantically identical (or nearly so) to a public right to know it.

The public only gained a broader legal right to access government information with the Freedom of Information Act, which was first enacted in 1966. Prior to that time, one could ask for information, but the government had no duty to respond. Since then, thanks to the FOIA, the public has had a legally enforceable right to compel disclosure of non-exempted information. As for the phrase "the right to know," it was apparently coined in the 1940s by Kent Cooper, who was the executive director of the Associated Press. The New York Times credited him with originating the phrase in an editorial on January 23, 1945. (As noted by James S. Pope in the Foreword to "The People's Right to Know" by Harold L. Cross, Columbia University Press, 1953."

To be sure, the public has access to criminal trials under the Sixth Amendment, but courts can conduct closed trials under certain circumstances. Criminal defendants are entitled to know the charges against them and have access to documents gathered by government in connection with the charges, but courts can address the relevancy of document requests. And we know grand juries conduct much of their work in secrecy.

In Florida, we have Marsy's law, which is designed to protect the privacy of victims of crime, but has been broadly interpreted to define who is and who is not a victim, leaving reporters and the public too often in the dark about information of public importance and of general interest.

The importance of an informed citizenry cannot be understated. Thomas Jefferson made it clear that a well-informed citizenry is the best defense against tyranny and is at the heart of a dynamic democracy. "Whenever the people are well-informed, they can be trusted with their own government." John F. Kennedy said "The ignorance of one voter in a Democracy impairs the security of all."

Throughout our nation's history, many have waxed eloquent on the vital importance of the public's right to know. Historians and legal scholars have argued throughout our history that the First Amendment's freedom of the press would have little, if any, significance if it weren't coupled with the public's right to know.

However, that right to know has never been deemed part of our Constitution; in most cases, the existence of this right is directly linked to the congressionally enacted Freedom of Information Act. Pointedly, the Supreme Court has never established a fundamental constitutional right for the public to know, either premised on the First Amendment right of a free press, or otherwise. It follows that unless there is such a right established by the Constitution, it is a "right" that is subject to legislative fiat that can be changed or eliminated. What this prospect says about the need for an informed citizenry to preserve our Democracy should be self-evident.

SHOULD POLICE BE PROTECTED FROM LAWSUITS UNDER QUALIFIED IMMUNITY?

As a result of recent cases involving police use of excessive force, much has been said and written about the doctrine of qualified immunity, a defense that protects them from liability for damages unless their actions violate clearly established law. There are efforts currently under way to have this defense either revised or repealed, thereby holding those accountable for their actions presumably in the same manner as ordinary citizens.

There are other forms of immunity from liability, however. I am not aware of any effort to revise or repeal these immunities. The fundamental question is whether, by office or occupation, anyone should be immune from liability for their actions that harm others and, if so, to what extent.

Books have been written on the subject of immunity. Here, I've tried to distill, without either overgeneralizing or omitting, key points for your consideration. And I've tried to eliminate as much legalese as possible. What appears below is culled from several sources, and my own experiences in defending government action, frequently relying on these defenses. The purpose of this narrative is to allow you to do your own research and form your own conclusions about the legitimacy of these doctrines in today's society.

SOVEREIGN IMMUNITY

Sovereign immunity is a type of legal protection that prevents the United States and its departments, as well as state governments and their departments, from being sued for money damages in the case of tort claims (injury claims as a result of negligence) without their consent. Sovereign immunity is found in the Eleventh Amendment to the United States Constitution and, in Florida, Art. X, Sec. 13.

This judicial doctrine was adopted from the law of England before Parliament rose to power. The idea was that the crown was above the people, and English subjects could not file civil lawsuits against the monarchy or its agents. In early American history, the United States couldn't be sued either by states or by citizens without Congressional approval.

Today, although waivers and exceptions have been legalized by federal and state legislatures that authorize certain civil suits against the government, sovereign immunity remains intact. The reasoning behind sovereign immunity

building of affordable housing in advantaged, majority-white neighborhoods and, thus, stymies racial desegregation efforts, so say the proponents. Books have been written on this subject, including "The Color of Law: A Forgotten History of How our Government Segregated America," by Richard Rothstein.

The essence of this approach is the relationship, or intersection. of race, zoning and other laws, and technology. Perhaps if racial issues were taught from fact only by viewing pertinent documents and engaging discussion, letting the audience reach their own conclusions, there would be a better understanding of what CRT is, as well as our history.

THE DIRE STATE OF ACADEMIC FREEDOM AT THE UNIVERSITY OF FLORIDA

If those three UF professors were retained as expert witnesses to testify in favor of Gov. DeSantis's position on voting rights, the university would have gladly encouraged and supported them--and probably would have earned them a pay raise or bonus. In a classic display of disingenuousness and gaslighting, UF contends it vigorously supports academic freedom--sure it does, so long as the exercise of that "freedom" supports the government's position.

Evidently, you can't upset the governor and his cronies-- who control funding of the state university system while monitoring campuses for academic freedom. Considering what the governor has done in blocking federal funds from paying the salaries of school board members who dared to put public health above political ideology, it's certainly no surprise in our Alice in Wonderland world where up is down, that the UF cancelled cultured these professors.

If these professors set out their positions in the classroom, no doubt one or more students would report them to the authorities, who would in turn take action against these malcontents. All in the name of academic freedom, of course. The UF administration should be ashamed of itself--but it isn't because it has convinced itself that it is acting in support of academic freedom. Down is up.

SHOULD PARENTS DICTATE TO SCHOOL OFFICIALS WHAT THEIR CHILDREN SHOULD BE TAUGHT?

I think most experts agree that education should prepare young people for life, work and citizenship. "Knowledge of the natural and engineered environments and how people live in the world is critical to all three purposes of education. Critical thinking, creativity, interpersonal skills and a sense of social responsibility all influence success in life, work and citizenship."

The government generally assigns this vital function in our democratic society to the local level; school boards, school superintendents, principals, teachers. Certainly, parents have a role in assuring that their children arrive at school prepared to learn, but having parents dictate to school officials what their children should and shouldn't be taught is a slippery slope, because what one group of parents might want, another vehemently opposes.

Education officials who must be elected are, of course, most sensitive to parental considerations. The important thing here is balance. If the focus of teaching comports with the definition set out above, we'll be fine. If, however, in what is increasingly becoming a topsy-turvy world, this definition is contorted by ideological rantings, then our form of government is at peril. Those in whose charge we vest the education of our children must keep this in the forefront of their minds.

UF ACADEMIC FREEDOM REVISITED

After refusing to allow three University of Florida experts to testify against the state's voting rights laws favored by the governor and Republican-led legislature, the university did an about-face today, saying they could testify so long as they aren't paid and don't use university time or resources. Evidently, the university believes that if these professors aren't paid, they won't testify.

But if they do, it certainly won't take much time or use of university resources, if any. These three are experts in their field; they already have the knowledge and experience to testify. And they can either take leave if they are to testify live, or by deposition when not on university time. And if they're not paid, it might be considered within the scope of their employment--for which they are paid--to serve as experts. It is to a university's credit that its professors have the expertise and competence to testify in court. I wonder if the university thought this through.

One of the first things that must be demonstrated in court is that the witness is in fact an expert in his/her field. To qualify a witness as an expert, a lawyer has the witness discuss his/her publications, university affiliations, and other scholarly matters. Presumably, these experts will testify to their status with the university, including writings published while on the faculty, and any other matter that deals with professional expertise. The standard for establishing expertise is not that high a burden. A university faculty member with particular knowledge, experience and expertise can easily meet that standard.

When cross-examining an expert, which I've done many times, a lawyer wants to show, among other things, some bias or prejudice by asking whether the witness is being paid. The purpose is to hopefully limit the value or impact of the testimony. The thinking here is that, obviously, if an expert is paid, he/she is being paid to testify for one side over the other, or so it goes. However, if an expert isn't paid, it can create the appearance that the testimony is unbiased and a matter of conscience--which is actually helpful to the side calling the witness. I wonder if the university considered this possibility.

To me, this looks like an effort to save face. The original decision, in the minds of many, struck a blow against academic freedom and free speech on university campuses. But if the university believes the problem is now solved, the administration had best think about the ramifications of this scenario.

THE UF'S DILEMMA ON ACADEMIC FREEDOM

The University of Florida has made national news, although for the wrong reason. A university is supposed to be the bastion of academic freedom and frees speech. Yet, administrators initially blocked three professors from testifying in a lawsuit brought against voting rights legislation favored by the governor and state legislature.

The UF explained that allowing these faculty members to testify in court would be in opposition to its interests because it must be seen as supportive of the government that funds and superintends public universities. In other words, the UF can't bite the hand that feeds it. In a classic display of disingenuousness and Orwellian logic--along with rank hypocrisy--the UF staunchly defends its role as a vigorous advocate for academic freedom. Sure it does, so long as that exercise is supportive of, and defers to, the government. Which, of course, means that, if academic freedom means the UF must genuflect to the powers that be, there really is no academic freedom. It is well established that academic freedom is a scholar's freedom to express ideas without risk of official interference or professional disadvantage. As one expert put it, "we cannot protect academic freedom by denying others the right to an opposing view"

But the UF, knowing it has backed itself into a corner, is now trying to weasel its way out by saying these professors can indeed testify, so long as they're not paid and don't use university resources. So, the gist of the latest iteration of the university's policy is these professors can testify against the voting law--and the university's interests in keeping the governor and legislature happy--so long as they aren't paid. Now, what does compensation have to do with the 180-degree turnaround of its position remains unexplained. Equally unexplained is how their testimony will keep the interests of the UF and the governor on the same page in keeping with university policy.

An interesting hypothetical question is, suppose these faculty members were being asked to testify in favor of the voting restriction law. Would the UF allow them to testify on their own time, for compensation, and use its resources? Is there a potential double standard here? I think we can guess the answer to these questions.

Evidently, these faculty members have previously testified as expert witnesses in other cases--with the UF's blessing, for compensation, on university time, and using its resources. There will no doubt be questions raised by the UF's previous actions against this new policy.

feckless attempt to save face, the UF will predictably appoint a committee to review policies on faculty testimony and how requests for expert testimony from faculty members will be handled in the future.

The smartest thing the UF can do now is to simply drop the matter. And any committee that is appointed should meet, take a few minutes to look at the policies that allow faculty members to testify as experts regardless of compensation, nod their heads in agreement that this is what academic freedom and free speech is all about, and adjourn the meeting.

In sum, don't make the black eye any blacker.

FOLKS OPPOSE SOCIAL PROGRAMS—UNTIL THEY DEPEND ON THEM

It's easy to rant about borrowing huge sums of money wastefully spent, but what exactly is an unnecessary social program? People thought social security was a wasteful program. Same for Medicare, Medicaid, Aid to Families With Dependent Children, etc. So, those of you who think the government is spending too much on social programs, please identify which programs you would eliminate, curtail, etc. And if you're receiving any social program benefit, would you agree to a reduction or elimination of that benefit.

It seems that those who oppose social programs only oppose those in which they don't participate or from which they receive any benefit. "Eliminate those programs that benefit them," seems to be the mantra. You won't hear someone say "please cut or eliminate those programs from which I receive benefits." This is much like the famous sign held at anti-social programs rallies that say "Hands off my social security." It's easy to oppose and rail against programs that don't affect you. Those who oppose these programs usually are of the attitude that it's ok to take from "them," but not from "me."

HISTORICALLY, WHAT IS A ZING! WHEN PUBLISHED IN A NEWSPAPER?

Each day, readers of The Tallahassee Democrat turn to the opinion page for the daily Zing!s If this column isn't the first one that's read, it's pretty close.

But lately, appearing in this column are such statements as:

"Go FSU soccer!"

"America's team wins!"

"Why are there so many acorns?"

"If you haven't seen the FSU Women's soccer team play, you are missing an amazing experience. Seriously. First round NCAA tourney: Friday 6 p.m."

thinking toward freedom of speech and press prior to and after the adoption of the First Amendment.

So, for all of those who are involved in zinging, you now know what a zing is.

WHAT DOES THE REPUBLICAN PARTY REALLY MEAN WHEN THEY CHANT ITS PARTY LINE

Over the years, the Republican Party has fancied itself as the party of limited government, lower taxes and family values. As shown by events over the past few years, this line is a myth. The Republican Party now toys with fascism, and is not shy about its authoritarian actions, particularly its anger at anyone who is different or has different views. The moderates have all but been driven from the party; its leadership now gives full vent to the far-right wing lunacy of Greene, Gaetz, Brooks, etc., with the leadership orchestrating the chorus by its silence or a shrug of the shoulders.

For limited government, the now far right-wing conservative party gives huge tax breaks to the big corporations and super-wealthy, still believing on the trickle-down myth; tells businesses they can't require patrons to wear masks, be vaccinated or offer proof of a negative test against a potentially lethal virus of pandemic proportions; takes issue with academic freedom on university and college campuses via a system of "thought police;" and on and on. Yes, they wax confidently on being champions of limited government--so long as businesses agree with them. If they don't, they will force you to agree with them.

For lower taxes, they refer primarily for the wealthy or super-rich. And whatever trickles down to the middle class is set to expire in a couple of years. While taking care of the wealthy, they oppose any program that's designed to benefit the greater general populace. They declare such efforts as "socialism," and their lemmings buy this, even while many are collecting their social security, Medicare, unemployment compensation, workers' compensation; and are not required to work more than a set number of hours, at a guaranteed wage and in a relatively safe environment. All of these are a result of Democrat Party (and liberal and moderate GOP members when they existed) actions against Republican conservative blowback.

The latest example of this is the infrastructure legislation. Our bridges, roadways and railways are deteriorating; have been for years. Yet, for the conservatives, it costs too much; it's a socialist giveaway, etc.; all the while, fighting like hell to prevent any increase in taxes for those like Donald Trump whose tax returns show he paid $750 in taxes over a couple of years, and no taxes in many others. No wonder he didn't want to disclose his tax returns. And, of course, it's not socialism to give tax breaks to the big corporations. For them, there's no such thing as corporate welfare, although we know there is.

For family values, the wax on liberty and freedom, confidently brandishing signs such as "my body, my choice" against masks and vaccines, yet deny this to women who want an abortion. They wave signs "keep your hands off my social security" which is the height of disingenuousness, assuming they know what that word means. They restrict voting rights under the laughable claim of eliminating voting fraud, which study after study reveals is virtually non-existent. I use these examples to show the myth of their family values mantra; I could go on and on about the hypocrisy of the "rigged election" lie and the January 6 assault on the Capitol, but the point is made—at least for those who haven't bought the Big Lie and don't believe that what happened in Washington was just some loveable supporters having a peaceful demonstration. The party of law and order has turned a blind eye to those "peaceful" demonstrators who attacked law enforcement and were looking to hang Mike Pence. In fact, they were called true patriots. And the nonsense continues unabated by those in the party who should know better. Are these examples of their precious "family values?"

I have asked Republicans to provide any facts that show that the conservatives have been on the right side of history. They were not on the right side of history when they opposed Franklin Roosevelt's New Deal, designed to get us out of the worst depression in our history. It was only after the Republicans were ousted from Congress that programs were passed that began to move the nation forward. Sure, it took several years, until the Supreme Court got on track, and certainly World War II finally moved our nation beyond the Depression, but it wasn't because of the overriding leadership of the Republican Party.

As isolationists, they were not on the right side of history when they opposed aiding Britain after Hitler invaded Poland and had his sights on greater conquests. They tied FDR's hands until Japan forced the GOP to join FDR and the Democrats in declaring war against them for bombing Pearl Harbor.

A few days after that, Germany declared war on us, and we reciprocated. But at that time, we weren't prepared for war, thanks to the isolationists. It took the most expansive mobilization effort in our nation's history to catch up and surpass the Axis's forces to win World War II. It doesn't take much to figure out what would have happened had the isolationists gained the upper hand.

The point here is to ask yourself the next time you hear the typical mantra of the conservatives opposing a program designed to help the average American that it's socialist or it costs too much, these questions: who are the beneficiaries of that program? How will that program affect me? Why can't the top 1 % pay more taxes than they do? And why can't the rest of us enjoy the same tax benefits the wealthy do?

A PROPOSED PLAN FOR THE DEMOCRATS TO GET THROUGH TO THE VOTERS

My dad taught me a long time ago not to talk a good game; if you see a problem, try to provide a solution. It's easy to point out problems; it's quite another to offer a suggested solution. So, taking to heart what Bill Maher said, and certainly recognizing it's not his job to offer solutions, here is my take on what the party should do. I am certainly not a party strategist, and there are those well steeped in history, politics and population dynamics who are far better at doing this, but I recall my dad's admonition, so here goes:

1. Describe what it means to be a Democrat. This should be a clearly worded statement of Democratic values and programs that help the vast majority of the populace.

2. Democrats should never shy away from saying they're proud to be Democrats. Use anecdotal information and examples from those who have benefitted over the years from Democrat-initiated programs.

3. For each program, describe in clear, concise sentences how they benefit the middle and lower classes, with emphasis on the workers--the Joe Buckets at the lunch counter; the construction worker sitting on the side of the road having lunch. Set out how each program helps in terms of dollars and actions.

4. Emphasize that the Republicans make noise and hand out labels, without proposing real programs designed to help the most people. They give huge tax breaks to the rich, but hand the rest of us crumbs, if even that.

5. When the Republicans assert their mantra of less government, less taxes, more freedom and liberty, and values, challenge them by showing how the deficit increased during Republican administrations; how tax reform actually benefitted the wealthy; how freedom and liberty doesn't apply to women or businesses acting for the general public health; and whether January 6's attack is an example of their values. Don't be reluctant to call out hypocrisy; whatever they dish out, they must receive in kind.

6. Repeat these messages.

7. Remind people over and over how the programs that benefit them and their families have, over history, been sponsored and passed by Democrats.

8. It's perfectly proper to list social security, unemployment compensation, workers' compensation, and other social programs passed by Democrats and signed by Democratic presidents.

9. Challenge the Republicans to identify those programs they passed that benefitted the majority of Americans over the years. Repeat this again and again.

10. Leadership is strength of conviction and positive assertions. Go forward with passion and confidence. Education takes time. Believe in the general goodness of people who eventually make those decisions that best exemplify our form of government that has been tested before and passed, is being tested now and must pass, and will no doubt be tested in the future. Our resiliency is what has guided us since our nation's founding. This is the stuff we're made of, not the noise and labels.

A PROPOSED PLAN: PART II

The media complain about the Republican message and that they're the "enemy of the people," yet they are the ones that helped create Trump and Trumpism. It won't be easy educating or re-educating those who've been stoked to anger and rage over the past few years, but the effort must be undertaken. Number 3 will require an extensive PR program that needs to begin yesterday. White papers are fine, if they're read. Thoughtful columnists, right and left. can write columns after columns, but they, too, must be read by the masses who've been conditioned to blindly accept the raging soundbites of the far right. As for the economy, take a page from the Clinton campaign. That slogan, "It's the economy, stupid" resonated. As for health care, focus on the number of people covered, those who are without health care, and the consequences of not having affordable health care.

I assume there are COVID statistics on this. Then, there are the bully pulpits. Biden has the loudest, but Pelosi and Schumer each have one. McConnell was a master at using it; Schumer not so much. Biden, Pelosi and Schumer need to fight fire with fire. When the Republicans make noise, the Democrats need to point this out. Republicans watch Fox News; the Democrats should take your advice and go on Fox News--and the other right-wing media as well. Democrats should have no trepidation about taking on right wing pundits. Now, whether the conservative media will allow them on is another matter. But that's another point they can emphasize. The more the Democrats press their points, the greater the prospect of the message resonating with those who feel alienated, or whose anger and rage have been thus far successfully aroused by the Republican rants and soundbites. Allowing lies and conspiracy theories to sink in without response is tantamount to allowing silence to counter them. That won't work.

HOW TO DEAL WITH CRITICAL RACE THEORY WITHOUT EMOTION

I think we can dispense with concerns over "critical race theory" rather easily in two steps. By all means, teach about history from the best available information. Teach about slavery, its history and practices. Include zoning laws; redlining.

Teach about the creation of the reservation, and how American Indians have been treated by our laws. Include laws that appear neutral on their face, but in practice discriminate by showing how these laws operate to discriminate, using facts, numbers, examples, etc.

Teach about how Japanese Americans were treated during World War II. Teach about how discrimination operates across the entire American spectrum. There is nothing theoretical about the facts of discrimination.

That is step one. Step two is to leave the moral judgments to others. Present the facts, applicable law and how they work in unison; let the audience reach whatever conclusions and judgments flow from the facts.

BOB DOLE: WAR HERO, FLAWED NIXON SUPPORTER POST WATERGATE

Bob Dole was certainly a war hero, and overcame much pain to serve his country long and well. But the one thing I hold him accountable for is his lauding of Richard Nixon as a hero, patriot and an all-American servant, without so much as a passing reference to Nixon's flaws.

No mention of Watergate; no mention of enemies' lists; no mention of attacks on the free press; no mention of attacks on peaceful protestors; no mention of resignation in the face of truth. Time certainly impacts how public officials are viewed, but we must never forget that unless we learn from history, we are condemned to repeats its harsh and frequently damning lessons. To be sure, we all have flaws; no one is perfect. But to ignore those serious flaws in public officials is to whitewash them or otherwise engage in revisionist history. And considering what recent history and current events tell us, we must never whitewash or dismiss those events for without that knowledge, we run the great risk of repeating them.

TRUMP AND CLINTON: WHO REALLY MIGHT JUST GO TO JAIL?

During the 2016 presidential campaign, then-candidate Donald Trump vilified his opponent, Hillary Clinton, over misuse of her email account, enticing his audiences with the intriguing question why she deleted 33,000 email. On the campaign trial, he repeatedly asked her, what are you trying to hide? and even invited the Russians to get to the bottom of this scandalous action.

Flash forward to today, and an appellate court's decision requiring disclosure to a congressional committee of Trump White House documents concerning the January 6 attack on the Capitol. While several Trump supporters have either ignored congressional subpoenas to provide relevant information in their possession, or provided tepid responses (and are all facing contempt citations and prosecution), Trump has vigorously resisted disclosure of those documents.

As a result of the appellate court's ruling, Trump now has one last shot to prevent disclosure, the Supreme Court. But those nine justices now face a dilemma: do they effectively protect Trump from what is in those documents and by doing so, give full voice to the belief that the Court is a political body even as some of its justices say otherwise? Or does the Court follow the time-honored and unbreakable legal chain that says the public is entitled to every man's evidence?

Several justices have come out publicly defending the Court from attacks of partisanship, saying while the justices have different approaches to deciding constitutional cases, those differences are of interpretative philosophies and are not political. Is the Court willing to take a hit to its reputation—a big hit--to save Trump from what he knows what will be revealed in those documents?

As other witnesses have come forward—and others are doing likewise--and documents are being turned over to Congress, Trump continues to resist, and is putting pressure on others who know the story of January 6 to resist as well.

The question Trump posed about Clinton can be pointed in his direction. Donald Trump, what are you trying to hide?

THE STATE OF JOURNALISM TODAY

Having graduated in journalism from UF, and spending a few years as a reporter in south Florida, I can certainly appreciate the changes that have taken place in news reporting. I think many of the changes stem from Watergate, and the eventual rise of advocacy journalism.

But today, when it's relatively easy to cast aspersions on journalists generally, the question that naturally arises is how does a reader (or viewer) determine what is fact over what is pure opinion or belief? There has to be some factual foundation for one to form a meaningful opinion. How is this possible if the news media in general is viewed with suspicion or disdain?

For me, I don't stick with one source. I read several newspapers daily, and watch more than one news network or newscast. I try to cull the facts from what I read and hear, and separate that from conclusory comments. For example, if a reporter informs that 200 people died in a conflagration, but then adds that Congress is lazy and has failed to do anything to prevent this horrible event from happening, I can easily separate the two.

Now, there may well be facts that will establish the cause of the event, and that Congress has failed to act, but that's for another day. The point here is that even as we might rail against the news media and its ethical underpinning (or not), we all form opinions. The key is on what foundation do we form our opinions---Opinion based on fact vs. opinion based on belief. Gathering facts and reaching informed opinions isn't easy; it takes diligence and hard work. Just like Democracy.

the government will never give journalists subpoena power. There are those who won't even acknowledge the power and authority of a congressional subpoena. As for lying, well, journalists have been calling out government lies since the nation's founding. Just keep it up; the liars can't stand the heat, and the result is a better-informed society.

BIDEN IS FROM THE FDR SCHOOL OF GOVERNMENT

Joe Biden is from the FDR school of government, believing that government exists to help the most vulnerable among us, and his policy initiatives reflect that. COVID wasn't created by him, nor what it fostered by his actions. In fact, he pushed hard to get everyone vaccinated and wear a mask in a concerted effort to bring down the appalling infection and death numbers.

And how were his efforts greeted? By vilification from the anti-vaxxers and anti-maskers as fomented by their leaders. The legitimate science tells us that these two measures will bring down those numbers; but because so many remain unvaccinated and won't otherwise follow public health measures, COVID remains with us, and will stay for at least the immediate future. This is on those who practice disinformation and misinformation, instead of steady leadership during an unprecedented pandemic. As for the economy, prices are generally set by demand.

As demand increases, so do prices. Biden doesn't set them. Gas prices are beginning to drop, and we can expect to see prices drop in other areas as well, but of course this will all be spun differently by the Trumpites, even as they do whatever they can to avoid accountability for their own actions. I realize that the Democrats have to do more than contend that the alternative is far worse than the status quo, but that doesn't resonate because it doesn't generate anger; and anger is what is fueling our governance these days. What the Democrats need to do is run on what passed, and how the Republicans have thwarted every other initiative.

Look at how the Republicans are now claiming credit for receipt of funds by the states--legislation that they vigorously opposed. They need to be called out again and again. The Democrats have been too timid, no doubt a result of Biden's efforts to negotiate and compromise. But today's Republican Party is not about compromise; it's all about winning the culture war at all cost.

HOW THE REPUBLICANS ARE TRYING TO DISTANCE THEMSELVES FROM JANUARY 6, 2021

In what has to rank right up there with the "rigged election" Big Lie, Trump loyalist Peter Navarro, in his book, tries to distance himself, among others, from the violence that occurred last January 6. He contends that he was an architect of a peaceful plan to pressure Vice President Pence to send the Electoral College votes of six states with Republican legislatures, back to them for the purpose of sending a different slate of electors that would vote for Trump.

In narrating this plan, Navarro wrote this: "Stephen K. Bannon, myself, and President Donald John Trump" were "the last three people on God's good Earth who want to see violence erupt on Capitol Hill... ."

Funny how these three peaceful men are now fighting like hell to avoid testifying before the congressional committee investigating the attack on the Capitol. They won't even provide documents to this committee.

It seems perfectly logical and proper to assume that if these innocent schemers had no hand in fomenting the violence, they would be eager to present their evidence to Congress.

But of course, we know why they won't cooperate with the committee. In the immortal words of Jack Nicholson, they "can't handle the truth."

But the bigger question is who, besides the fiercest Trump loyalists, actually believes this latest claptrap?

THE CHUTZPAH AWARD FOR SHEER GALL

Today's chutzpah award for unmitigated impudence and gall goes to Gov. Ron DeSantis. While COVID cases surge in Florida to record highs, what is our governor doing? Aside from being out of sight along with his surgeon general, he's busy blasting AOC for daring to remove her mask so she can eat and drink in a Miami restaurant. Talk about trying to deflect from one's own failings! This does nothing for him, except energize his base by scapegoating the "enemy" in the form of a New York congresswoman.

In a blatant effort to embarrass those who criticized his absence for the past two weeks as COVID cases surged in Florida, Gov. Ron DeSantis said he was accompanying his wife for cancer treatment. The outrage among his ardent supporters was immediate; how dare anyone criticize him for caring for his wife!

But wait just a second here. No one is criticizing him for caring for his wife. What the critics are saying is that why, for two weeks, he couldn't find five minutes to get before a camera and assure an anxious citizenry that he has everything under control?

Why couldn't he couldn't pick up the phone and direct the surgeon general to go public with necessary assurance? If you have ever accompanied a loved one for treatment, you know it doesn't take every waking moment over a two-week period to accomplish that. If indeed he really needed two full weeks to do this, he could have directed the lieutenant governor to handle things in his absence. He did none of this; he went AWOL. He knows his excuse will play to his base; it won't play to his critics simply because there are too many holes in his story that remain to be filled.

A PRESIDENT'S ROLE AS CONSOLER-IN-CHIEF

One of the most important roles of a chief executive is consoler-in-chief or assurer-in-chief. No one was better at these roles than FDR. He certainly took his share of vacations--Hyde Park, Warm Springs--but during times of crises--and he had many--he was never far from the radio. So, by way of analogy, while it's certainly holiday season, that is no excuse for choosing to be off-media during a public health crisis, especially after seeking out publicity to engage in self-praise. And if he wanted to be out of the public eye for whatever reason, political or otherwise, then at least designate those to speak in his stead to calm the waters and provide reassurance. He didn't do any of that. I didn't get to finish my previous post, but your initial post asked what I would have done. I wouldn't have sought the media's attention to praise myself during good times, and then do a disappearing act when things went south. And I believe you wouldn't have, either.

HOW DEMOCRACY DIES

Whether, as the Washington Post says, "Democracy dies in darkness," or, as some historians note, Democracy dies "by a thousand cuts," the common theme is a dystopian one: the death of this grand experiment in self-government. As January 6 approaches, it is essential that we reflect on what transpired in Washington D.C. one year ago, and how close we came to the unthinkable.

Democracy's downfall won't arrive with a grand pronouncement, and it won't happen overnight. It will arrive cloaked in the nation's flag. It will be ushered in by public officials. It will promise freedom, liberty and the rule of law. It will enter federal, state and local governments. It will enter the legislative, executive and judicial branches of government. It will enter the military and law enforcement. It will enter our colleges and universities. It will enter our local school systems.

In the name of reform, it will re-write constitutional law, making illegal what is now guaranteed. It will pass laws to deal with non-existent problems. To deal with perceived problems, it will create draconian solutions. In the name of liberty, it will restrict liberty. In the name of freedom, it will restrict freedom. And it will define rule of law to mean whatever fits its mindset.

In the name of less government, it will expand control over lower forms of government. Facts will take a back seat to belief. Lies will be offered as truth; truth will be lies. Science will be rejected. History will be re-written. Traditional Democratic institutions will be demeaned and attacked. Books will be banned; curricula will be cleansed and controlled. Ideology will prevail.

It will create a scapegoat, accusing "them" of fearmongering; branding them as radicals, extremists, Anti-Democratic, "enemies of the people," etc. Those who dare to point this out will be castigated, silenced or worse. Fear, anger and blind acceptance will replace reason, logic, critical thinking and common sense. Gradually, the flag will unfurl, revealing one word emblazoned on its chest: Fascism

---

FEELING GREAT AT 78

Today is my birthday. I am now 78 years old. I share this birthdate with Christine McVie of Fleetwood Mac fame, and Julius Caesar. There's a message here, but I won't dwell on it. For having reached this august milestone (in July), I was gifted with a free package of hearing aid batteries. There's a message here, too. I think most folks who make it to this age experience some ology, or ist, or ics. I fall into one of these categories: orthopedics.

Tomorrow, I see a neurologist for my quarterly Botox injection in my neck, courtesy of spinal fusion surgery 10 years ago. Over the years, I have had both knees and one shoulder replaced, and need the other one done, as well. It's one thing for family and friends to call me the Bionic Man; it's quite another when my orthopedic surgeons call me that. But I feel I've earned this title because over the years, I have kept several surgeons and an entire orthopedic clinic fully funded (thanks to my insurance provider) and operational (no pun intended).

I have had more than two dozen surgeries on my foot, hands, shoulders, back (upper and lower). I take medication for pain and soreness, but I am constantly reminded that my specialists are orthopedic surgeons, not oncologists, cardiologists, rheumatologists, or other doctors who deal with serious conditions. My orthopedists remind me they can patch me up and send me on my way. Those who must deal with other medical disciplines are not as lucky.

I figured that over the years, I could have been the beneficiary of my parents' millions, or their arthritic conditions. Since they didn't have the former, they gifted me with the latter. And that's really ok, considering the alternative. Neither of my parents made it to 79; both passed away at 78--which is why this birthday has greater significance.

But I plan to spend this year--and beyond--being thankful for what my life has given me. A fantastic wife, two magnificent daughters, two great sons-in-law, and four incredibly smart and precocious and wonderful grandchildren. And my 90-year-old great-uncle Joe and cousins as well. And thanks to DNA and perseverance, a niece, nephew-in-law and three grandnieces. Professionally, my years as a newspaper reporter and 50-year member of The Florida Bar have given me much to appreciate and give thanks for. So what if I have to take Aleve or Flexeril or Tylenol or Crestor or even a COVID booster shot now and then. I'll take all of that gladly, and give thanks for the gift of a remarkable life that keeps on giving. So, Happy Birthday to Me. The best is yet to be!

WHEN DEMOCRATS AND REPUBLICANS WORKED SIDE BY SIDE

I just read an illuminating history of the post WW II era (from 1945 to 1949) entitled "Harry and Arthur," by Lawrence J. Haas. Although published in 2016, it is in stark comparison to the relationship between the Democrats and Republicans today, particularly in a divided Congress. The book tells of the relationship between Harry Truman and GOP Senator Arthur Vandenburg of Michigan. Although a staunch isolationist, Pearl Harbor convinced Vandenburg that isolationism would not serve America well in the future. So, together Truman and Vandenburg worked to usher in a new world order consisting of the United Nations, the Truman Doctrine involving aid to Greece and Turkey to keep them from Stalin's influence, the Marshall Plan to revive the European economy after so much of that continue lay in ruin, and the North Atlantic Treaty, which led to the creation of NATO, where an attack on one member nation was an attack on all. After reading this book, I give pause to wonder what the post-war world would have looked like had Vandenburg not taken it upon himself to work with Truman and, instead, stonewalled or obstructed rebuilding efforts.

JANUARY 6, 2021 WAS NO PATRIOTIC ACT IN DEFENSE OF DEMOCRACY, NO MATTER HOW THE REPUBLICANS TRY TO SPIN IT

Does anyone really believe that what happened a year ago was a patriotic act in defense of Democracy? Let's face it; we've always had strains of bigotry, be it based on race, religion and national origin, but those who spew such bile always were on the fringe, outcasts and relegated to the sidelines.

What has happened is that elected officials, starting with Trump and moving to Lindsey Graham, Mitch McConnell, Matt Gaetz, Marjorie Taylor Greene, Paul Gosar, and on and on, have given aid and comfort to those January 6 insurrectionists by labeling such treasonous conduct as patriotic. To be sure, there is nothing patriotic about attacking our principal institutions of government.

People can certainly disagree with government policies; in fact, they can even believe the "rigged election" Big Lie, but when they engage in violent acts designed to overthrow a constitutional function of our government, and attack the very symbols of our nation, particularly based on belief and lies, the line has been crossed. Those officials who continue to support Trump's Big Lie and, in doing so, give cover along with aid and comfort, there is only one word that accurately describes this. And it isn't patriotism.

There should be no surprise here. While we certainly have a pretty good idea of what transpired, as soon as the truth is fully made known, the insurrectionists and those who, in the name of law and order, enabled or gave them aid and comfort will be exposed for what they are. What we do with this information is quite another story. No doubt, the accomplices and their ilk will double down on their conspiracy theories and Big Lie claims; they'll accuse Democrats, as well as Independents and Republicans who remain true to their party's traditional conservative principles, of being Anti-American, socialists, etc. We all know their playbook; they repeat its contents over and over again ad nauseam. Three realities must come from this: first, we must all realize that this horrible conduct doesn't represent the traditional Republican Party.

Even past party faithful have come out in visceral opposition to what took place a year ago. These accomplices highjacked the GOP and turned it into something else, something antithetical to our Democratic form of government. Second, opposition to those who planned and executed this attack on our government must be loud, vigorous and unceasing. They must be called out for what they are, and those who continue to support this scofflaw behavior must be embarrassed to the point of returning to the caves from whence they came.

Being tepid in response to this only aids the attackers, accomplices and their acolytes. Third, they must be prosecuted to the fullest extent of the law. Provisions must be made for continuing full speed ahead even if the investigation isn't concluded and the Republicans gain control of Congress and shelve the investigation--which we all know they will. This is dangerous moment in our history; there is no time for silence or timidity. The tools are available in our Constitution and federal law to weed out those who would undermine our 250-year-old experiment in self-government. Just as tools are used to build and repair, so must our legal tools be used to fix what is perilously at risk of breaking beyond repair.

WHEN A POLITICIAN WHO OPPOSES POLITICIZING IS PART OF THE PROBLEM

Predictably, Gov. Ron DeSantis calls yesterday's anniversary of one of the darkest days in our history "nauseating" and "politicized."

"It's interesting how everything in our society becomes very politicized," he added.

But hasn't the governor been at the forefront of politicization of issues that bend to his mindset, and that of his fellow Trumpites? Example: Just over six years ago, he railed at Hillary Clinton, calling her emails a "national security disaster." I wonder if he remembers that? How has history treated his rant since then?

The so-called email scandal wound up as a big nothingburger, except for getting Trump elected. No one was charged, there was no trial, and the matter disappeared, even though his party had control of Congress and the White House. I wonder if he remembers when Trump said Clinton should be in jail. He certainly said it often enough. Maybe not, but if there were a real case, you can bet a united states attorney appointed by Trump would have prosecuted. Didn't happen.

But things are different now. As much as he would like January 6 to be forgotten, it looks rather glum for his party cohorts and fellow groupies as investigations close the ring tighter and tighter around his political guru and Trump's obedient lemmings.

I can well understand the governor's deference to Trump; after all, he elected him by giving him the endorsement he needed four years ago. But treating Clinton's situation as a major national crisis while hoping folks ignore what happened last January, and yesterday's commemoration of that horrible attack, well, quite frankly, it doesn't pass the smell test.

His comments yesterday reek of hypocrisy he accuses Democrats of fomenting. But I can also understand his statement yesterday that Floridians are more concerned about gas prices, inflation and education than an insurrection. Funny, you left out COVID, but considering his handling of that, I can understand why.

It's all about deflection. People have short memory spans and the hope is that by election time, enough people will forget about the seditious attack and move on.

But, you see, January 6 has now joined December 7 and 9/11 as days of the most despicable attacks on our country. And just as the first two days of infamy are etched in our nation's history, so will January 6 with this difference: the first two were attacks by non-Americans; the attack last year was launched by Americans against their own government. Surely, you can recall your condemnation of this shortly after it happened. What changed? Oh, yes, it's election year and Trump remains the all-powerful. You certainly don't want to incur his wrath.

But history tells us that sooner or later, uneasy relationships turn sour as ego takes over. Friends soon turn on one another. And the clock is ticking.

THE PARTY OF LAW AND ORDER HAS A PROBLEM WITH LAW AND ORDER

On the subject of party popularity, here's another matter that deserves consideration. The Republicans fancy themselves as the party of law and order, yet many elected Republican officials oppose any inquiry into events leading up to, and following, the January 6 attack on our Capitol. Governor DeSantis just appeared before Florida law enforcement.

If he is such a strong advocate for law and order, why does he oppose holding accountable those who aided the attack on our Capitol last January 6? The attackers assaulted law enforcement officers. If he believes in law and order as he and his party faithful assert, why is he against holding responsible those elected officials who aided the assault? And why does he oppose the Congressional investigation into that assault?

If he claims it's a partisan investigation, how does he explain two members of Congress from the Republican Party who are on that investigative committee? Doesn't he want to get to the bottom of that attack? Doesn't he want to find out why law enforcement officers were brutally attacked and injured? And why did he assail Hillary Clinton for her email, calling her actions a national security breach, yet he would have us ignore January 6? Is there a legitimate difference, or is it a matter that, for the now-configured Republican Party, law and order applies only to others, not to them?

IS VOTING A RIGHT OR PRIVILEGE?

There has been so much said and written about this subject since the 2020 election that it deserves a fresh look now, particularly since many states have recently enacted voting laws premised on avoiding fraud. This article answers this question with this answer: it depends. Democrats generally view voting as a fundamental right; Republicans generally view voting as a privilege. I find this not surprising, but disappointing.

The reason for this is that in four amendments to our Constitution, these words appear: The right of citizens to vote... ; Whether the particular issue is one of race, color or previous condition of servitude (15th Amendment); sex (19th Amendment); poll tax (24th Amendment); or age (26th Amendment), the right to vote is so well established that these amendments simply assume the obvious; well, at least obvious to a majority of Democrats and a minority of Republicans. Interestingly, the Supreme Court has never declared voting as a fundamental right based on a confluence of these amendments and their historical settings. Perhaps the day will come as more and more of voting restrictions make their way through the judiciary when voting will be firmly found to be a fundamental right inherent in a Democracy.

THE ONLY THING NEW IS THE HISTORY YOU DON'T KNOW

It was President Harry Truman who said "The only thing new in the world is the history you do not know." This reiterates the adage that history is cyclical and repeats itself. From this, it follows that those who do not learn history's harsh lessons are doomed to repeat them.

In the late 1930s, as events were unfolding in Europe and President Franklin Roosevelt wrestled with a possible third term candidacy, he faced growing criticism of his New Deal as well as his foreign policies, most vigorously from the right. During this time, William Richards Castle, Jr., an American diplomat who joined in this criticism, is reported to have said "When Democracy denigrates into socialism a form of dictatorship of the right is better for the nation."

To discern what he meant, we need only look to events that were capturing the world's attention at this time—the leadup to World War II in Europe and the rise of Fascism and Nazism.

Dictionaries that deal with historical subjects generally define fascism as a system of government led by a dictator who typically rules by force, often violently suppressing opposition and criticism, controlling all industry and commerce, and promoting nationalism and often racism.

As an ideology, fascism typically centers around extreme nationalism and an opposition to democracy and liberalism. In practice, fascism revolves around a ruler who uses absolute power to suppress the individual freedom of citizens, making everyone completely subject to the power of the state. To achieve this, fascism often uses violent methods for political ends. In the context of a fascist government, this often involves the use of the military against citizens.

Nazism is defined as one type of fascism. Both fascism and Nazism reject democracy and liberalism as ideologies, and instead embrace the concept of a nationalist state.

Fascism as an ideology focuses on the state itself. However, fascist leaders typically gain support by appealing to people's nationalism and racism, especially by promoting suspicion or hatred of people that they label as foreigners or otherwise cast as illegitimate citizens—as Hitler did with the Jews in Germany. Such leaders often reinforce these themes among their followers with rallies and mass parades (developing what's sometimes called a cult of personality).

Nazis (today's movement to revive Nazism is also known as neo-Nazism) believe in the superiority of the Aryan race. Nazis embrace such concepts as eugenics (which discouraged, for example, "reproduction by persons having genetic defects or presumed to have inheritable undesirable traits") and scientific racism to further their views. Nazism views the state as a means to perpetuate these racist views.

With specific reference to totalitarianism, it was Joseph Geobbels who said "Repeat a lie often enough and it becomes the truth."

From Castle's ominous statement, it is not a leap of logic to conclude that all that is necessary for this line of thinking to gain traction is to convince by repetition that the "socialism" rant is true, and that there is really no other choice but a form of dictatorship of the right.

Of course, this presupposes not taking into account the fact that our nation has had a form of socialism since the 1930s with FDR's New Deal. From 1933 to 1939, either through legislation or executive orders, major federal programs and agencies were established to address our dire economic condition, including the Civilian Conservation Corps (CCC), the Civil Works Administration (CWA), the Farm Security Administration (FSA), the National Industrial Recovery

Act of 1933 (NIRA) and the Social Security Administration (SSA). They provided support for farmers, the unemployed, youth and the elderly. It's called Democratic Socialism.

To this, we can add Medicare and Medicaid, and the recent infrastructure and COVID-related legislation, among others.

But as long as the "socialism" rant remains in the forefront of our political discourse shorn of any careful and complete explanation, Castle's stark statement from our past echoes in the wind.

THERE IS NOTHING HIDDEN ABOUT THE REPUBLICAN PARTY'S AGENDA ANYMORE

I give the Republican Party (or more accurately, the right-wing extremists who have commandeered the party) credit for being entirely aboveboard in their plans should they recapture Congress. The putative House leadership, in the form of Kevin McCarthy and Jim Jordan, has vowed to remove members from their committee assignments (McCarthy) and impeach President Biden (Jordan).

McCarthy vows to remove three Democratic House members in retaliation for Pelosi's removal of two Republican House members. Specifically, he said he would strip Democratic Reps. Adam Schiff and Eric Swalwell, both of California, and Ilhan Omar of Minnesota, of their committee assignments. Schiff and Swalwell serve on the

House Intelligence Committee, while Omar serves on the House Foreign Affairs Committee.

Recall that several months ago, House Speaker Nancy Pelosi stripped Paul Gosar of Arizona and Marjorie Taylor Greene of Georgia from their committees for inflammatory rhetoric and posts. Gosar was censured and removed from his committee seats for posting a photoshopped anime video to his Twitter and Instagram accounts showing him appearing to kill Democratic Rep. Alexandria Ocasio-Cortez of New York and attacking President Joe Biden. He eventually took the post down but retweeted a tweet that contained the video hours after being disciplined by the House. Greene, meanwhile, was stripped of her committee assignments in the wake of incendiary and violent past statements that had been unearthed shortly after she was sworn in.

Against this backdrop, what exactly did the three Democratic representatives do to deserve removal from their committees? Here is a classic example of deflection from McCarthy: "The Democrats have created a new thing where they're picking and choosing who could be on committee. Never in the history have you had the majority tell the minority who could be on committee," McCarthy lamented in an interview with Breitbart.

McCarthy's attempt at some measure of equivalency, however, is bogus.

We know that the two Republican engaged in inflammatory rhetoric and posts. For moral or functional equivalency, McCarthy said Schiff "lied to the American public" with his support of the unverified Steele dossier, which alleged extensive ties between former President Trump and Russia.

He pointed to Swalwell's association with a Chinese spy, reported by Axios. Swalwell, who cut ties with the spy after being alerted to her activities by federal investigators, has not been accused of wrongdoing. In the case of Omar, McCarthy quoted her 2019 remark that a pro-Israel lobbying group's influence in Congress is "all about the Benjamins," which was blasted by members of both parties at the time as anti-Semitic.

You can decide if what Greene and Gosar did is in any way equivalent to what McCarthy conjured up to exact his revenge. Suffice it to say that if every little peccadillo justified removal from one's committee assignments, I doubt if many in Congress—including McCarthy and Jordan—would be serving on committees, and certainly not speaker of the House. I suppose they are overlooking that statement about letting those without sin cast the first stone.

Continuing his deflection, however, McCarthy said "[House Speaker Nancy] Pelosi has set new policies here. Those same members that I talked about in my speech … voted for these new policies," alluding to Schiff, Swalwell, Omar and Democratic Rep. Maxine Waters, also of California.

"This isn't about threats, but it's about holding people accountable."

His claim about new policies is similarly bogus. The fact is there are no new policies at play here; it's simply a matter of sanctioning House members who behaved in a manner that is beneath the dignity of the office of United States representative. More to the point, however, is that according to McCarthy, it's perfectly ok to hold these three Democratic House members "accountable," but accountability doesn't apply to members of his own party, most notably Gosar and Greene, and former President Trump for that matter.

We can add some other Republican members of Congress as well; their behavior will eventually come out of the wash in the form of Congressional and other investigations. McCarthy shows great hubris in holding Democrats accountable, while simultaneously thumbing his nose at a Congressional investigation designed to get to the truth behind the January 6 assault. To paraphrase a recent former president: what is he trying to hide?

McCarthy's strained attempt at justification for his promise doesn't pass the smell test.

There should be no doubt underlying McCarthy's and Jordan's promises: retaliation for removing two Republican representatives for outrageous and dangerous behavior, and impeaching Biden for daring to defeat Trump at the ballot box and Electoral College. Recall that Schiff led the House impeachment effort; Swalwell and Omar voted to impeach.

Biden refused to protect Trump's papers from being disclosed under the former's ludicrous claim of executive privilege pertaining to potential criminal conduct.

Jordan, for his justification, said Biden "is not fit for the job. He hasn't done anything right." If that were the test for impeachment, why didn't he vote in favor the last two times? We, of course, know the answer to that.

There is no doubt this is the beginning of a purge of those who dared to hold former President Trump accountable for (1) seeking a foreign government's assistance in his re-election campaign; and (2) instigating an insurrection on our Capitol at a time when officials were performing the constitutional duty of certifying the presidential election.

To be clear, these are violations of federal law. But to those who now promise House committee purges and a presidential impeachment, reasons don't matter. It's all about pleasing Trump and his ardent followers--and exacting revenge.

Lest you think this is all in isolation and not part of a disturbing pattern, the Republican National Committee has now informed the Commission on Presidential Debates that the committee's candidates won't participate going forward. I suppose you can't have party candidates appear foolish, uniformed and downright stupid on live television.

The Republican Party has no need to hide its agenda anymore; they can now be open and aboveboard about their playbook, because they believe that enough people believe in what they are selling as Democracy.

THIS IS OUTRAGEOUS CONDUCT FROM A UNITED STATES SENATOR

Republican Senator Josh Hawley of Missouri said he would not have supported a resolution honoring the work of Capitol personnel on the anniversary of the January 6 riot at the U.S. Capitol because it described the attackers as "violent insurrectionists."

The tens of millions who saw the videos on that day of infamy know that the Capitol was attacked to stop the constitutionally mandated certification of the 2020 presidential election. Five people died in that attack; dozens of law enforcement officers were assaulted and injured; the building itself was damaged; and some of the participants were looking for Mike Pence and Nancy Pelosi, among others, to attack them.

Against this backdrop, what language would Sen. Hawley have preferred to call those who attacked this major symbol of our Democracy?

Perhaps he would have been happy if the resolution referred to those who stormed the Capitol as simply a "meeting of merry marauders." Or perhaps a "pack of prayerful protesting peaceniks." How about a "bunch of braying brats?" A "collection of costumed clowns?" Maybe "narrow-minded Neanderthals."

Let's see if we can help Sen. Hawley, despite his denial, deception and deflection.

Violence is defined as "using or involving the use of physical force to cause harm or damage to someone or something; trying to physically attack someone because of anger."

Insurrection is defined as "an act or instance of revolting against civil authority or an established government." Insurrectionists are those who take part in an insurrection.

Those who saw what unfolded just over a year ago saw "physical force causing harm or damage" by those who, in trying to stop the election certification process, acted in revolt of civil authority or our established government. But evidently not Sen. Hawley. It is obviously impossible for him to come to terms with this reality, because it cuts against his ideology and blind support for his guru.

What is sad, and scary, is that he was elected to one of the highest offices in our nation. And in the 21st century.

Although it's been about 300 years since the start of the Age of Enlightenment, it is quite obvious that there are those who still wallow in the ignorance akin to the Dark Ages.

WILL THE FINAL REPORT ON JANUARY 6 MAKE WATERGATE LOOK LIKE A PICNIC IN THE PARK?

Today's column by Historian Heather Cox Richardson is a must-read for those who want to come to terms with how perilously close we came to a takeover of our constitutional form of government.

If Richardson's comments represent only a portion of what the Congressional committee, which is investigating last year's attack on our Capitol, concludes in its final report, it will make Watergate look like a picnic in the park.

We have a fairly good idea now of what transpired from what is already in the public record. Much more will be forthcoming, despite the stonewalling and hollow claims of partisanship by Trump's acolytes. Recalling words from a famous movie, it seems they "can't handle the truth."

In her column, Richardson discusses the difference between voter fraud—which is virtually non-existent and which would have had no effect on the 2020 presidential election—and election fraud which Trump and his cabal came dangerously close to pulling off, and would have succeeded had a few not held tight to our constitutional norms. Even for them, what Trump and cohorts wanted was too much to stomach.

Capsulizing this nefarious scheme, the core of the plan was to have the Republicans choose alternate slates of electors in seven states won by Biden. Ultimately, these seven alternate slates would be chosen by then-Vice President Pence over the duly elected delegates, or he would simply reject counting the slates won by Biden, thereby in either case declaring Trump the winner in the Electoral College. If there was a dispute, the plan called for sending the election to the House of Representatives where each state gets one vote, and the Republicans hold 26 of the states, making Trump the winner this way. For a third prong, the dispute would wind up in the Supreme Court where Trump expected loyalty from its conservative members and thereby declare him the winner.

Fortunately, a few otherwise Trump loyalists refused to go along with this nefarious plan. Then-Attorney General Bill Barr called the "voter fraud" claim bogus; a few in the Justice Department refused to go along with this election steal, and VP Pence opted to protect the integrity of our election process by refusing to take part in this assault on our government.

Hard-core Trump loyalists will no doubt cast aside Richardson's findings of fact as "misinformation," or "fake news" or some other choice shorthanded method of dismissing inconvenient truths—just as they dismissed the Mueller Report on Trump's dealing with Russia; his first impeachment for seeking a foreign government's help in his re-election bid; and his efforts to stoke the fires for the assault on Congress the purpose of which was to stop the presidential election certification process, which led to his second impeachment. As you read Richardson's column, ask yourself why are so many of Trump's loyalists refusing to testify before the Congressional committee? When Trump was campaigning against Hillary Clinton, he asked her why she hadn't testified about her handling of email while secretary of state. He intoned famously: "what is she trying to hide?" Of course, she did testify under oath, and no charges were ever brought against her even when Trump was president who appointed all 93 united states attorneys. and both houses of Congress were in Republican hands.

So, to ask the question Trump asked Clinton, why haven't you testified? Why are you and your minions balking at testifying? What are you trying to hide? From the public record gleaned thus far, We kinda sorta know.

The better angels in our country are desirous of getting to the truth behind the assault. The vast majority of Americans want the truth to come out, as it did in Watergate and other scandals that have rocked past presidential administrations. To be sure, it will come out in the January 6 investigation; we all know the truth has a stubborn way of coming out. What we do with it is really the key here. Our nation can't afford for that report to simply gather dust on the shelf. You all know the adage about those who fail to learn the harsh lessons of history.

FLORIDA GOVERNOR AND CONGRESSIONAL REDISTRICTING; HOW DID WE GET HERE?

Republican Gov. Ron DeSantis has taken the unusual step of inserting himself into the redistricting process by submitting a proposal to reshape Florida's congressional map and carve up districts held by Black Democrats.

This is a move that should surprise no one who is familiar with the redistricting process that takes place every 10 years after the census is taken.

What Gov. DeSantis is now intending to do is in effect reverse engineer what began back in 1992. Adopting the view that Republican congressional districts that surround majority Black districts are relatively safe even if more Democratic voters are added, he wants to dilute those majority Black districts by moving some voters into those surrounding districts. This would make those districts harder for Blacks and Democrats to hold onto, while assuring that those surrounding districts remain in Republican hands.

An example of the stark reality that is our polarized politics, just this number serves as the introduction to my discussion here: in the United States Senate, the 48 Democrats and the 2 Independents who caucus with them together represent 40.5 million more people than the 50 Republicans do. In the House, the Democrats have 222 members, the Republicans have 212. However, by national percentages of voter registration, Democrats have 49 million, Republicans have 36 million, with 30 million registered as Independents.

How did we get to where we are? This is central question that undergirds the many discussions on politics posted on Facebook. Commentators and pundits declare that we are a divided nation politically and ideologically. We have seen extremism play out, most recently and graphically on January 6 last year. How did we get here?

As a lawyer back in the 70s to 2010--and during that time having been involved in voting rights and election cases-- including reapportionment and redistricting of legislative seats, term limits, and having a part in the 2000 presidential election--I have my own opinion on how we got here. So, here is my take, with the understanding that in trying to accomplish this is as short a narrative as possible, specific details are sacrificed. However, this should provide a good overview of what transpired over the past few decades.

Elections have historically been the subject of state regulation. Over the years, the Jim Crow-fed, state-by-state disparities in voting eligibility requirements, coupled steps taken to physically prevent access to polling places— particularly as they affected minorities—led to the passage of the 1965 Voting Rights Act. That law provided, among other things, that any voting practice, procedure or standard that impacted minority participation in the electoral process was a violation of federal law. Section 2 of that law provided that a violation can be established if it can be shown that the intent of the legislation was to discriminate.

However, discerning the intent of a legislative body proved to be an almost impossible standard to reach. As a result, Congress in 1980 changed the standard of proof necessary to prove a violation of federal law to one of effect or impact, and the Supreme Court in 1982 said that if it can be shown, through statistics and other data, that the effect of a voting provision adversely impacted minorities, that established a violation of law requiring remedial steps be taken by government to correct it. Last year, however, the Supreme Court effectively gutted the import of Section by upholding Arizona's voting restrictions passed in the wake of the 2020 presidential election. The Court's vote was 6 to 3, and it doesn't take a rocket scientist to discern how the six conservatives or the three liberals decided the case.

(Another section of the Voting Rights Act, Section 5, required certain jurisdictions to submit to the U.S. Justice Department any voting or election change that might adversely impact minorities. This provision was declared unconstitutional by the Supreme Court in 2013.)

Now for the next part of this explanation. Reapportionment and redistricting of congressional House seats and state legislatures take place every 10 years following the latest census, which takes place in every year ending in 0. (These seats will be rearranged during this legislative session since it follows the 2020 census.)

The first time the state legislatures undertook this process since the Court's 1982 decision was in 1992, following the 1990 decennial census. That year, the push was on by both Democrats and Republicans to deal with this law as interpreted by the Supreme Court. (Reapportionment means the reallocation of congressional House seats according to population. If a state's population drops, it will lose seats to states that have experienced population growth over the previous 10 years. Redistricting is how districts are created once population figures are determined following the decennial census. All seats must be as near to population equality as possible. Over the years, technology has made the population variances among districts almost non-existent.)

The party in power in the legislature controls the redistricting process for both congressional and state legislative seats. Since congressional districts are based on population, when the population shifts, some states lose seats and others gain, while the total number of House seats remains fixed at 435.Based on the 2020 census, Florida adds another congressional seat, bringing the number to 29. Remember the first rule of politics is survival; the second is perpetuation.

Packing and Bleaching Districts

1992 was the first time the Supreme Court standard for dealing with the creation of representative districts was addressed following the 1982 Supreme Court decision

the state by the feds. Not to mention socialism, a dictatorship and other pejorative terms the party faithful cavalierly toss around whenever they dislike something that government is trying to do.

But over the strong objection of cities and counties, a Florida House panel has approved a measure that would give businesses a right to sue when a local ordinance hurts their bottom line. The measure would create a cause of action for businesses if a local ordinance or charter amendment reduces the business' revenue or profits by 15%. Some restrictions would apply, but its purpose is unmistakable--control over local governments through fear and intimidation.

The view that local governments have home rule to decide for themselves what is in the best interests of their citizens is sadly going down the drain. For those in state government, it's perfectly ok to dictate and control what local governments do; but it's horrific for the federal government to do the same thing to the state.

Rank hypocrisy aside, it is evident that for the state's Republican Party, what is good for the goose (the state) is not good for the gander (the federal and local governments). Just another part of the party's playbook—do whatever they want in the name of liberty, freedom and reform. As long as their voters buy it, the party will continue to sell it.

WHEN NEUTRAL APPEARING LAWS DISCRIMINATE IN PRACTICE

When discussions on Facebook turn to the subject of voting restrictions passed by several states in the wake of the 2020 presidential election, numerous posters ask essentially the same question: what exactly are those restrictions? Another way of asking this question is how can a law restrict if it applies to all equally, without reference to any group? These questions are facially plausible, until the practical realities are addressed.

Here is the reality.

When Congress passed the Voting Rights Act, it recognized that laws that appear neutral on their face can operate to discriminate when historical voting patterns and voting burdens placed on some groups over others are considered.

On the general subject of neutral policies that nevertheless support institutional racism, see https://info. newjerseyattorneys.com/how-seemingly-neutral...

With specific regard to voting laws that are discriminatory in practice, see https://scholarlycommons.law.emory.edu/.../ viewcontent...

These are just two articles that address this subject. There are, of course, many more. Reviewing legal research articles can be a daunting task for laypersons; lawyers, too, but they do explain how laws neutral on paper can discriminate in fact by way of their operation.

It is well understood among scholars that from the perspective of political parties, the purpose of elections is to win. Common sense dictates that. Winners get the rewards; political power to implement their policies and ideologies. "To the victor go the spoils."

When elections are fair, every voter has equal access to the polls, and every legal vote is counted legally. But if there are ways that voting, and counting votes that appear equal on paper, can nevertheless be manipulated in fact based on how people vote, why wouldn't a political party take advantage of this in order to gain and maintain power?

These types of advantages that one group has over another lie at the heart of the Voting Rights Act, and the Supreme Court eventually recognized this. In 1982, the Court eliminated the need to show intentional discrimination in favor of an evidentiary standard that requires only a showing that a neutral appearing law can have a discriminatory or disparate impact on one group over another. Thus, 40 years ago, the Court recognized that requiring proof of intentional discrimination imposed a nearly impossible burden. Instead, the Court recognized that a standard of proof requiring demonstration of a discriminatory impact by statistical data is far more reasonable and practical in search of the truth of discrimination.

But most recently, that changed when the Court approved voting restrictions passed by Arizona in the wake of the 2020 presidential election. Several states passed laws under the false rubric of eliminating voter fraud by targeting how certain groups vote and making it harder for them to exercise that right and have their votes counted equally with others. What caused this change? The composition of the Court changed.

But the Voting Rights laws that were on the books 40 years ago remain today, although eviscerated through interpretation by the Court's current makeup. Obviously, a change in the Court's makeup will affect how the law is interpreted. But that's for another day. The purpose of this brief note is to make readers aware that (1) that there are laws that on paper apply equally to all, but (2) how these laws actually operate in the real world can discriminate by giving some groups advantages over others.

"VISION WITHOUT EXECUTION"

Do you have experiences with people who profess to having good ideas but expect others to implement them? This is one of my great pet peeves. I have had folks tell me what wonderful ideas they have. When I advise them to offer a plan to implement them, starting with their leadership commitment, they quickly back off, saying they're simply the idea person, fully expecting others to the work to implement them.

To them, I say if your idea isn't worthy of your efforts at execution, you are actually saying you're too lazy to be bothered putting your idea into operation. If you think your idea is really unworthy of your time, then keep it to yourself. "Vision without execution is hallucination."- Thomas Edison

With revelations pouring out on a daily basis, it is becoming clear that it was former President Trump and his cohorts who conspired "to overturn the election and undermine our democracy." And now, with the Supreme Court having given a green light for the House Select Committee Investigating the January 6 assault on the U.S. Capitol to gain access to Trump's presidential papers—papers he vigorously sought to secret from the committee and the public—we can expect even more graphic revelations to come forth.

REPUBLICANS MAKE A MOCKERY OF CONGRESSIONAL INVESTIGATION BY INVOKING FIFTH AMENDMENT

From what historian Heather Cox Richardson is discussing today, it may not matter whether those who have ignored or snubbed their noses at congressional subpoenas ever testify. They would only plead the 5th Amendment if they were ever compelled to appear anyway.

The fact is that with more and more witnesses with first-hand knowledge of what transpired now talking to the committee and providing documentary evidence, the committee will have more than enough substantial concrete evidence to conclude what is becoming increasingly obvious: an elaborate, far-reaching plot involving rejection of duly chosen electors and their illegal replacement by fake electors in seven states as part of a scheme that tramples on our Constitution. From lawyer John Eastman's letter laying out the White House plan to overturn the election by requiring unconstitutional acts (he plead the 5th Amendment when called to testify), to Fox News commentator Sean Hannity's January 10 text to Rep. Jim Jordan saying "we have a clear path to land the plane in 9 days," the web of deceit is untangling.

And this is not the only investigation Trump is facing as the walls continue to close in on him and his acolytes. Stay tuned.

WHAT IS HISTORY?

History is about the human experience; a continuous never-ending search for truth through accuracy. It is a constant dialog between the past and the present. Recognizing that the record is written by the fallible, every effort must be made to glean the facts to the best of our abilities. The facts must be studied with all of its warts and imperfections. Those in the present can only learn to do better and be better if we understand the past; its successes as well as its failures. Indeed, we learn more from mistakes than successes. History must not be watered down or altered to placate or please any group or individual. Its teachings must not depend on hurt feelings or particular sensibilities. Viewing history through rose-colored glasses is viewing a lie—a lie to ourselves. We simply don't learn by choosing to live a lie.

JOURNALISM ETHICS: A DOUBLE STANDARD?

Former CNN Host and lawyer Chris Cuomo was fired because he wasn't forthcoming in providing legal assistance to his brother, former New York Governor Andrew Cuomo, when the latter was facing charges of sexual abuse. CNN, in terminating Cuomo, cited a breach of journalism ethics.

Fox News commentator Sean Hannity remains employed and on the air despite revelations as to his involvement in efforts to overturn the 2020 presidential election. Recently disclosed text messages turned over to the congressional investigation committee make it clear that Hannity was aware of exactly what was happening — including the bizarre attempt to get Vice President Mike Pence to overturn the election — and he worried that White House lawyers might resign en masse. Clearly, Hannity was a player, certainly not acting like a journalist.

Further, in a January 10, 2021, text to Republican Congressman and Trump loyalist Jim Jordan—four days after the attack on the Capitol--Hannity said "we have a clear path to land the plane in 9 days." What exactly did he mean by this?

Was Hannity aware that there was a plot hatched in the White House involving rejection of duly chosen electors and their illegal replacement by fake electors in seven states? We also know that the congressional committee has a lengthy letter from lawyer John Eastman laying out the White House plan to steal the election for Trump (Eastman plead the 5th Amendment when called to testify). Was he also aware of this?

As noted previously, Hannity was certainly aware of a nefarious scheme to overturn the election. What remains is the true depth of that awareness. But from what we know so far, the question naturally arises: why is Hannity still employed? Why has he not at least been suspended pending a full investigation?

Is Fox News even conducting an investigation into Hannity's involvement in this plot? Has Fox News made any comment regarding this?

Cuomo was fired for helping his brother. Hannity is still employed despite involvement in a scheme to overturn a presidential election by nefarious means. From this, are we to conclude that it is ethically permissible to participate in an unconstitutional, anti-democratic effort to steal an election, but it is not permissible to assist a brother in his defense?

For CNN, it was about journalism ethics. What about Fox News's journalism ethics? Perhaps it really doesn't have any.

THREE HISTORICAL TIPPING POINTS, AND THE ONE WE FACE TODAY

The Trump White House documents that he vigorously sought to keep secret have now been turned over to the House committee investigating the attack on the U.S. Capitol on January 6 of last year. From the disclosure of one document mentioned yesterday but published in full today, we can expect further, perhaps even more stark and shocking revelations.

This one document is a blockbuster, and it is essential for the preservation of our Democracy that you take heed and pay attention.

According to reports in Politico and by Heather Cox Richardson, it is an unsigned executive order dated December 16, 2020, just two days after the false Trump electors in seven states executed documents falsely saying Trump had won the election in their states. The executive order falsely claims that there is "evidence of international and foreign interference in the November 3, 2020, election."

Those complaints were used to justify using the National Guard to seize the nation's election machines. Read that line again.

The order told the secretary of defense to "seize, collect, retain and analyze all machines, equipment, electronically stored information, and material records" from the election.

It gave the defense secretary power to call up the National Guard to support him and told the assistant secretary of defense for homeland security to provide support from the Department of Homeland Security.

The secretary of defense had 60 days to provide an assessment to the Office of the Director of National Intelligence, suggesting that the process would continue after Inauguration Day.

The executive order also provided for "[t]he appointment of a Special Counsel to oversee this operation and institute all criminal and civil proceedings as appropriate based on the evidence collected and provided all resources necessary to carry out her duties consistent with federal laws and the Constitution."

(Do you see the irony here? Donald Trump intended to engage in the most intrusive possible federal interference in state elections. This, from the leader of a party that just killed a voting rights bill on the alleged grounds it was federal overreach.)

The House committee will no doubt uncover who was behind this plot, this effort at a coup, Sidney Powell's name being more prominently mentioned. While we are indeed fortunate that cooler heads talked Trump out of issuing this executive order, it doesn't take much of a reach to conclude what the outcome would have been.

We are at an historical tipping point that must not and cannot be met with silence or timidity. This particular tipping point is more like a fork in the road, requiring us to make a fundamental choice as to which road we want to take. History is our guidepost, and we must pay heed.

To be sure, we've faced tipping points before. We faced one early on in our history when, after fighting to gain our independence, George Washington chose to be a term-limited president rather than replicate the monarchy we fought against. He shepherded our fledging nation through its birth years. We can only speculate what our nation would have become had he not opted for a limited term chief executive, and acted more like a monarch than a president.

Abraham Lincoln faced it when he put all his energies into preserving our union, as Americans fought Americans over state's rights against the promise of equality under the law for all, meaning all. He well recognized that "a house divided against itself cannot stand." Again, we can only wonder what America would have become had there been a different result.

Franklin Roosevelt faced tipping points from two sources, domestically through an unprecedented crisis that tested the economic foundation and social fabric of our nation, and a brutal world war that, had the allies not won, America would be a far different country today.

Those major crises, however, occurred when our nation was still going through early growing pains. In 1789, our nation's population was 3.4 million. In 1861, it was 31.4 million. In 1933, it was 125.5 million, and in 1941, it was 133.4 million. Compare these numbers to our current population of 332.9 million. Much of rural America is now urbanized, and urban centers have become megalopolises.

Today, we are the most diverse America in our history. People from every major continent live and work here. They raise their families here. Look to nations north, south, east and west, and we have people whose ancestors came from those countries and made this their country, just like our ancestors did. Whether Oriental, African, European, Asian, South American, really shouldn't matter, because we all share one thing in common: we're all Americans.

But we know there are those who believe that being an American requires some pecking order; a belief that there can only be one superior group, with the others necessarily inferior.

History speaks to us loudly today. Are we listening?

It tells us the Civil War was fought over the issue of state's rights as pressed by the South, and slavery as pressed by the north. Vestiges of that time remain with us today.

It tells us the World War II period similarly contains elements of the conditions that inform of the tipping point we face today.

It tells us that in the late 1930s and early 40s, America was primarily an isolationist country driven by an American First mentality. You may recall that the America First Committee, a non-interventionist, isolationist pressure group formed in 1940, lobbied Congress against American involvement in foreign wars, specifically against American entry into World War II. The group was one of the largest antiwar organizations in the country with 800,000 members at its peak. This committee emphasized American nationalism and unilateralism in international relations. It also opposed broad immigration, with particular emphasis on Jews trying to escape from Hitler and his "final solution." Its slogan was America First.

(Does this ring a bell? "America First" was the official foreign policy doctrine of the Trump administration.)

During this period, there were influential Americans both in and out of government who steadfastly resisted helping Britain when it faced Hitler's advances, and even urged our government to negotiate with Hitler. National hero Charles Lindbergh was at the forefront of Americans urging negotiations. He certainly wasn't alone.

Of course, December 7, 1941 and declarations of war involving Japan, Germany and Italy, quieted the America First isolationists, and the committee quickly disbanded. Yet even during the war, the undercurrents of America First were so embedded in our government and nation that it constrained Roosevelt from dealing more forcefully with

Hitler's atrocities. History also teaches that the war didn't permanently silence those America First voices.

Today, we see a strain of America First nationalism again. We hear it in speeches from the far right, replicating the themes from the past. Stoked by an authoritarian leader, we hear the message most clearly. Anti-immigration. Anti-Semitism. Racial superiority. Underlying religious fervor. Lies being sold as truth. Truth being called lies. Suppression of major guardrails of Democracy. And on and on.

Fortunately, the stark truth about what actually transpired before, during and after the January 6 attack on the Capitol is emerging. It is now time for accountability and individual responsibility. As more and more information is unearthed, it is important to remember that, in a den of thieves, there is no honor. Members will turn on one another to protect themselves. And that will advantage our Democracy.

As these investigative processes move forward, it is important--indeed, essential--that we pay attention. Sitting on the sidelines is not an option. History is cyclical because it's steeped in human nature, and unless we are vigilant and vocal, history will once again repeat itself. And this time, with a diverse nation of more than 330 million, the consequences could well be unthinkable.

LET'S JUST PASS A LAW

It's so easy to legalize illegal, immoral, unethical, even horrific conduct. Just pass a law. Then, in defense of the indefensible, all that need be said is "It's the law."

Current legal conduct upsets you? Laws you don't like, don't want or just bother you? We'll just pass a law and do away with this.

All that is necessary to rile up the mindless followers is to create an "enemy" that supports laws and conduct that make you angry, sad, embarrassed, or evoke any other emotion that simply annoys you. Once the masses are on board, it's a quick hop-skip-jump to the adoption of a law that will bring you happiness and joy—or at least this is how the new law will be sold.

Of course, this new law will be offered as an example of freedom and liberty. It may even be called a reform measure. Regardless, it will be couched in comforting words that are designed to make you happy--facts and critical thinking be damned. It doesn't matter how the law operates to harm others, and it doesn't matter if the laws restrict, suppress, undermine or abolish democratic principles and guardrails, so long as passing and enforcing them makes you feel good. In the words of that wonderful tune: "Don't worry; be happy."

History is replete with examples of laws designed to do away with conduct that those in power don't want, don't like and otherwise go against their ideology. And millions have died in the name of "It's the law."

The most graphic are the Nuremberg Race Laws passed during Hitler's first year in office. https://encyclopedia. ushmm.org/content/en/article/the-nuremberg-race-laws

Ah, yes. How easy it is to rid yourselves of undesirable laws—and people. Just pass a law.

REPUBLICANS KNOW THAT ANGER SELLS, ESPECIALLY IF PACKAGED AS FREEDOM, LIBERTY AND JUSTICE

While the Republicans package their "freedom, liberty and justice" rhetoric is an "I'm mad as hell and I'm not going to take it anymore" platform, the Democrats can't seem to find a note that either excites their supporters or rings a bell with the "disaffected." The Republicans realized years ago that anger sells.

Getting people riled up and emotional sells. It's not a leap of logic to realize that when you're angry, you want to do something about it. Like participate in get-out-the-vote drives, as well as other organizations designed to translate anger into policy. I don't know whether the Democrats can change; they've been relying on the old Roosevelt plan of federal involvement into the affairs of its citizens for almost 100 years now.

At various times, that worked. But since Reagan said "the problem is government," things have changed. Biden's low ratings should be a strong sign that passing major legislation alone isn't enough. While he has to deal with intransigence within his own party, which is no fault of his, and some missteps (Afghanistan withdrawal and COVID response), which are, it seems that whatever he gets passed; indeed, whatever he does, simply doesn't seem to matter.

Of course, we can certainly debate whether what the Republican Party is doing on abortion, academic freedom, classroom curriculum, voting, public health and safety; etc., is best for the country, but with each movement by the party--and the country--further to the right, there doesn't appear to be a concerted voice of wisdom that can successfully counter it. The Democrats seem hellbent on doing the same things over and over again, expecting a different result. This, of course, is the classic definition of insanity.

MESSAGES FOR US FROM THE TWILIGHT ZONE

If a survey were conducted today of the most influential people in the history of the mass media, I doubt the name of Rod Serling would appear. Yet, during each holiday period, you will find his most well-known works on the Sci Fi channel: "The Twilight Zone." What makes Serling so influential even today is the messaging he used in telling his stories.

For those of you familiar with the series, you will no doubt recall the eerie theme song leading up to each of the 156 episodes aired from 1959 to 1964 on CBS, 92 of which were written by Serling. You will recall his brief narrative openings:

"You're traveling through another dimension -- a dimension not only of sight and sound but of mind. A journey into a wondrous land whose boundaries are that of imagination. That's a signpost up ahead: your next stop: the Twilight Zone!

You unlock this door with the key of imagination. Beyond it is another dimension: a dimension of sound, a dimension of sight, a dimension of mind. You're moving into a land of both shadow and substance, of things and ideas. You've just crossed over into... the Twilight Zone.

There is a fifth dimension beyond that which is known to man. It is a dimension as vast as space and as timeless as infinity. It is the middle ground between light and shadow, between science and superstition, and it lies between the pit of man's fears and the summit of his knowledge. This is the dimension of imagination. It is an area which we call "The Twilight Zone"."

You will recall his brief lead-in monologue explaining what is about to be aired, concluding with the ominous sounding words "the Twilight Zone."

Serling was called a visionary, a man ahead of his time, for his poignant social commentary. What made this series so great was its take--through clear and crisp writing and stark visuals--on human nature, the human condition, and the consequences of not taking heed of our fears, anxieties, weaknesses, prejudices, etc.

Through re-rums, his messages remain with us today. Our challenge is to apply them to our present circumstances.

For those unfamiliar with Serling's work, Each episode of this American anthology horror series presented a stand-alone story in which characters find themselves dealing with often disturbing or unusual events, an experience described as entering "the Twilight Zone," often with a surprise ending and a moral. Although predominantly science-fiction, the show's paranormal and Kafkaesque events leaned the show towards fantasy and horror. The phrase "twilight zone," inspired by the series, is used to describe surreal experiences.

Although offered as entertainment, some episodes were designed as a dystopian warning to make the viewer think. Those familiar with the anthology will recall such episodes as "The Monsters are Due on Maple Street," "The Obsolete Man," "Eye of the Beholder," "The Masks," "To Serve

Man," "The Invaders," and "Time Enough at Last" among many other starkly thematic episodes.

The Twilight Zone is widely regarded as one of the greatest television series of all time.

HOAXES, WITCH HUNTS AND DENIALS

The battle over academic freedom on our college and university campuses, and over curriculum in our schools, has far more sinister consequences than might first appear.

We can readily agree that the core purpose of education is prepare for a productive life in a dynamic society by developing skills that maximize creativity, interpersonal skills. Additionally, education instills a sense of social responsibility which influences success in life, work and citizenship. The ability to analyze and engage in critical thinking is essential for the development of the mind. We know that uninformed disengaged citizens lead to poor policy choices that adversely impact life, work and citizenship. In short, "if you think education is expensive, try ignorance."-Derek Bok, president of Harvard University.

If freedom of expression depends on pleasing government officials; if certain subjects are off-limits; if what is taught depends on comfort level; if books can be banned based on personal feelings, then it should be self-evident that what is sacrificed is knowledge. But make no mistake about it, it's the sources of our knowledge that lie at the heart of these culture battles. There are two: science and history.

We can address science rather quickly. Although there are those who deny climate change and critical aspects of medical science, they can't deny what is around them. Violent storms. Strange, persistent increasingly violent weather patterns. Major flooding in places not previously known to have severe floods. Wild fires raging out of control. A raging pandemic that is about to enter its third year. Despite the efforts of some to hide their heads in the sand, there can be no credible denying of these and other related violent climate and weather events.

History is an entirely different matter. History provides knowledge of the past to help us live in the present and prepare for the future. It follows that denying history denies knowledge, while rewriting history provides false knowledge. If we don't teach history with all of its imperfections, it will be impossible for future generations to learn history's harsh lessons; consequently, those harsh lessons will be repeated. Simply put, how can we learn from history if it is not taught, or taught in a false light?

In the absence of the search for truth, emotion and passion reign supreme. Without knowledge, it becomes easier and easier to brand inconvenient truths as hoaxes, uncomfortable allegations as witch hunts, and allows for plausible denial. How easy would it be to call something a hoax or witch hunt—and have the masses believe it-- without knowing history?

Today, we bear witness to how these words were used over the past few years to reject or castigate rather than enlighten. You can look to your local news and these words will invariably appear. If the search for knowledge is stifled, or cut off, each successive generation, not exposed to these truths, will simply deny them, or call them hoaxes or witch hunts without any foundation or frame of reference.

Genocide makes you uncomfortable, or the powers-that-be don't want it taught? Just call it a hoax. How about the Holocaust? Just another hoax. Race relations in the United States are not harmonious? Oh, we can't teach that; that might make some folks feel uncomfortable. Think of history's most horrific conflagrations and how things would be going forward if they weren't taught.

How about letting parents decide the school's curriculum? What could go wrong with parents fighting over what can and can't be taught, and what can and can't be read! Are we as a supposedly enlightened people to allow books to be banned, burned, or buried in caves and underground? Are we to allow curriculum to be cleansed of all references that cause discomfort or pain?

Of course, these draconian decisions assume all parents can agree on a single curriculum. Perhaps we will wind up with a two-headed school system, where one curriculum is available to one group, and a cleansed curriculum devoid of the uncomfortable available to the other. The impact of this on the necessity of a unified school system should be obvious.

Educators are taught pedagogy, or how to teach and how children learn, on a professional level. Presumably, parents take the time to learn about child-rearing and some basic learning skills, but there's no requirement. There is a wide difference between pedagogy and parenthood, however. Parents certainly can and should have input; in fact, they do just about every day when they see their child's grades and reports, and when they visit with the teachers. But leave education to the educated and trained educators; having parents decided curriculum is flat-out dangerous, if for no other reason than one parent's good idea is anathema to another.

BECOMING INFORMED IN AN ERA OF INFORMATION OVERLOAD

My take on this is, assuming some or most or all of this is true; what is to be done about it? Are the points Wilson makes the resulting inevitability of doing nothing? And what specifically should be the role of the media in informing the electorate, knowing that a sizeable chunk seems to have no problem with where the Republican Party wants to take the country?

Journalists are trained to be unbiased; to present the facts and let the audience reach its own conclusions. But how do reporters remain unbiased and silent in the face of the clear and unvarnished promises being made by the right once they gain power, as they expect to do in this year's midterm elections, and beyond?

There are fairly comprehensive statements out there as to the proper role of a news reporter; generally, reporters are responsible for gathering and disseminating important information, and delivering updates and analysis on current happenings with the main goal of keeping the public informed.

Notice the word "analysis." Shouldn't a reporter provide analysis along with the cold, hard facts to provide context, meaning and significance? Considering what Wilson says—and he is by no means alone—what is to be made of the traditional role of the reporter as a gatherer and chronicler of facts? Reporters steeped in history, government, civics, law, etc., have opinions formed from their education and experience. As they gather facts from their respective frames of reference, are they to keep this mix of knowledge and experience to themselves in the face of assaults on our governmental structure, with promises of more to come? Isn't one of the purposes of having reporters gain expertise on various subject matters like schools, government, crime, etc., to provide context along with facts? Should the traditional fact-gathering role of the reporter be revisited in light of the times we now live in, and what might well lie ahead?

I think we understand the threats and promises. I think we understand the rank hypocrisy of, in the name of freedom and liberty, stomping down on voting access, quashing academic freedom, banning "uncomfortable" teachings from school curriculum; I could go on and on about other anti-Democratic acts that have been thrust on the nation, with more to come.

WHEN HAVE CONSERVATIVES BEEN ON THE RIGHT SIDE OF HISTORY?

But again that refrain: what are we to do about it?

This is the question that I have been asking every time one of these types of comments are posted: When have the conservatives been on the right side of history? Supporting slavery in the name of states' rights? NO. Supporting laissez-faire free economics at the turn of the 20th century? NO. (Remember the Great Depression?) Supporting Social Security and other New Deal programs designed to bolster a depressed economy to get us out of the Depression? NO. (The Republican Party is about big business, not the individual.)

How about their support for isolationism and America First during WW II? NO. (When Pearl Harbor was attacked, we weren't ready for war. Thankfully, the Democratic administration of FDR got us ready in time.) Supporting Medicare, Medicaid and Voting Rights legislation in the 1960s? NO. (The Republicans have historically opposed government involvement in public health, and we all know their stand on voting rights.)

How about government ethics? NO. (Remember Watergate and Iran-Contra?) Trickledown economics? NO. (Businesses are not designed to spread the wealth to the workers. They are in business to make money, and the more the merrier.) How about their relationship with labor and the right for groups to organize for health, safety and welfare purposes? NO. (The Republicans are for big business, but will fight every effort to allow for even close to a level playing field for laborers.)

This is a good summary of the Republican Party over the years. And today? Well, they oppose voting rights, academic freedom, teaching history with all of its warts and failings, home rule for local governments (but scream bloody murder when the federal government tries the same approach to the states; and on and on. Again, they continue to be on the wrong side of history.

They claim they're the party of Lincoln and believe in freedom, liberty and individual responsibility. Except that the current version of the party is anathema to Lincoln. Except that in the name of freedom and liberty, they continue to deny it to the greater mass of the population. In the name of individual responsibility, they are trying mightily to have you forget what happened last January 6 when the Capitol was attacked, even stonewalling or ignoring legitimate investigations.

Did I mention their claim to be the party of law and order? Well, remind them of that attack by their supporters on dozens of law enforcement officers during that fateful January 6 insurrection....which they even refuse to acknowledge was an assault. They can continue to deny, deflect and delay, and they can certainly convince some of the people some of the time, but they can't fool all of the people all of the time. The truth has a stubborn way of eventually coming out. And it will come out.

REPUBLICANS' RELIANCE ON FALSE EQUIVALENCIES

Whenever something like this is published, the right immediately seeks out a functional equivalent, as if whatever the far right does, the far left does the same, so they are equally to blame, equally at fault. Case closed; move on. Nonsense. This is a false premise, resulting in a false analogy.

There are degrees of extremist conduct that must not be cavalierly dismissed by reliance on "whataboutism." When Newt Gingrich says congressional investigators might be jailed for doing their job, there is nothing from the far left that is functionally equivalent. When the far right promises to derail investigations into criminal and quite possibly treasonous conduct by public officials--and others--there is nothing functionally equivalent on the far left.

When the far-right excuses Trump's conduct, but is hellbent on making investigators pay for daring to conduct the juvenile, time-worn, woefully overused and bogus "witch hunt," there is no functional equivalency here. Whether you love the far right and damn the far left, or vice versa, weighing the facts such as the nature and type of crime--which lie at the core of our criminal justice system--destroys any credibility of a functional equivalency claim. While it certainly gives comfort to those who rely on it, it's ultimately a vacuous claim that provides a false sense of security.

It wasn't the far left that attacked the Capitol--including law enforcement officers--yet somehow the far right equates that assault that took five lives with attacks on businesses during racial protests. To be sure, both are extreme measures, but they are not functionally equivalent. An assault on one of our fundamental Democratic guardrails--the peaceful transfer of power following certification of a presidential election--finds no functional (or moral) equivalency in burning a McDonald's in protest of racial inequality.

Yes, by all means, both are intolerable. Both are crimes. But they are most assuredly not equivalent. If one robs a bank and the other person kills people, both are certainly crimes. But they aren't functionally equivalent. Do you know why we have differing degrees of penalties for different crimes? Because one size doesn't fit all in our criminal justice system; each one is different, with different degrees of severity matched by different levels of penalties.

Those who burned McDonald's will answer to our criminal justice system; and so will those who fomented, led and participated in the attack on the Capitol. That's the way it works in a Democracy "if we can keep it."

OBJECTIVITY BY SUBJECTIVE PEOPLE

It never ceases to amaze me how people can reach diametrically opposite conclusions after viewing the same event. The most glaring recent example of this is what transpired on January 6 at the Capitol in Washington, D.C. Whether that was an insurrectionist attack on our government, or simply a few diehard political supporters acting a bit overzealously, the overriding fact is that both views are vigorously defended by their respective advocates.

Why is this so? Shouldn't objective facts easily support one conclusion over the other—one that we can all agree on? Perhaps therein lies the problem.

You see, we are imperfect beings, with emotions, biases, prejudices, beliefs; indeed, possessive of all of the human characteristics—strengths and weaknesses—that are inherent in the human experience. We are the sum and substance of our education, training and experiences.

When we see or hear something, that information goes through that subjective, imperfect filter, and produces an opinion or belief that is in line with those imperfections. And yet, to reach a rational, logical conclusion that reflects a consensus, we are urged (or should be urged) to be objective in our reasoning.

Simply put, a subjective perspective is a more personal, emotional, possibly impractical point of view, where one's perspective is based solely on personal biased, emotionally imbued views. An objective perspective is the opposite; objective perspectives are based on facts/statistics--things that can be proven, with no personal bias. This is why the emphasis is on objective inquiry.

Of course, a purely objective viewpoint is harder to reach because as humans, we are subjective beings, no matter how objective or "open minded" we claim to be.

The ultimate question, however, is whether we are capable of elevating our thinking to the objective, because the search for objectivity is essential if we are to achieve agreement or consensus that is essential to our form of government.

The journalism profession is steeped in the search for the truth. Reporters are educated and trained to seek out objective facts and report them to the public so that they can make reasoned, informed decisions.

Our judicial system is based on a search for the truth; that is, an objective search for those facts that lead to a consensus or, in some instances, required unanimity. This search is premised on the well-established view that objective viewpoints yield more acceptable results because they are fact-based and hence, more reliable.

Assuming the worst, how will authoritarianism come to America? And what will it look like when it arrives?

At the outset, it will not arrive with tanks and loaded weapons. It will arrive cloaked in the American Flag, accompanied by cries of patriotism and promises of freedom, liberty and law and order.

The more nuanced question, however, is what seeds must be planted to assure an authoritarian takeover.

Here is my take.

First, both houses of Congress must be in the hands of the extreme right wing of the Republican Party. Moderates within the party must be rendered ineffective, voiceless.

Second, the president must be a Republican who favors authoritarianism.

If these two conditions are met, the Republican Party can then get rid of the filibuster and pass just about any legislation it desires. Further, control of judicial appointments is with the Republicans, and a president can appoint like-minded lawyers to the Supreme Court and all lower federal courts, where the vast majority of cases are decided.

Once these two conditions are met, the Republican Party then controls the federal government; with the length of such control allowing for systematic removal within government of career Democrats, replaced by Republican party faithful.

The Democrats will thus be rendered ineffective, their voices meaningless.

By the late 2020s, if Republicans elect and re-elect a president representing the far- right wing, and Congress goes through four straight off-year elections with Republicans in control, it doesn't take a stretch of the imagination to see what the nation will look like politically, socially or culturally, at the turn of the next decade.

To achieve this level of success, however, the party must succeed at the ballot box. This is accomplished by doing as much as possible to suppress the Democratic vote. Fully aware of historic voting patterns, Republican majorities in the state legislatures can pass laws that make it much harder for Democrats to vote. Any challenges arrive in courts presided over by judges appointed by Republican governors. Where the legislatures are controlled by Republicans, overriding Democratic gubernatorial vetoes is possible.

Of course, Democrats' efforts to supersede these suppressive laws at the federal level run into a wall in Congress, and the outcome of any court challenges going before federal judges appointed and confirmed by Republicans, should be self-evident.

Any of this ring a bell?

But there is an even more sinister plan, one that can upend how we currently choose our president. This is the third are deflecting or avoiding accountability for that assault, and how many remain silent as the Big Lie rant continues. These are just a few examples; there are, of course, others.

Within the last couple of days, Trump's Secretary of State Mike Pompeo praised Russia's Putin even as the latter is about to invade the Ukraine.

Of course, the easiest thing to do is to simply say "it can't happen here," or treat this narrative as pure fiction. For the sake of our country, I hope you're right. But what if you're not?

A REPRESENTATIVE DEMOCRACY?

Last night, 48 senators who represent 182 million Americans, 55% of the United States population, supported allowing voting rights legislation to advance to floor debate and vote by rejecting application of the filibuster to this particular issue, while 52 senators who represent 148 million Americans, 45% of the country, voted against it by supporting the filibuster. That's a population difference of 34 million. To those who believe that in a Democracy, majority rules, take a look at these numbers again. And while you're at it, take a look at the history of the filibuster, particularly as it has been used to block civil rights legislation. Historian HEATHER COX RICHARDSON discusses this and other issues, particularly the Trump White House papers on January 6 now cleared by the Supreme Court to be turned over to the House Committee investigating the riot, and

Trump's plan to run for re-election in 2024 based on the Department of Justice's ruling that a sitting president can't be charged or put on trial while in office. Another most interesting read.

FLIPPING THE SCRIPT ON DRACONIAN THOUGHT CONTROL LEGISLATION

The other day, I posted an article on a law's unintended consequence. Perhaps I was erroneously giving the Florida Legislature the benefit of the doubt. Maybe the consequences are in fact intended to produce a draconian result.

The law in question is a proposal targeting Critical Race Theory. However, I asked the question whether it would end there. This proposal, if enacted into law, would prohibit individuals from making people "feel discomfort, guilt, anguish, or any other form of psychological distress on account of his or her race, color, sex, or national origin." Considering how broad this proposal is, I asked what other forms of teaching, what other courses in an academic curriculum, would or could create "psychological distress" in any person?

Rhetorically, I asked about how this definition of "psychological distress" would affect teaching about the Holocaust. How would it impact any discussion of genocide, ethnic cleansing or any related subject, since these are about one group claiming superiority over another based on "race, color, sex, or national origin?" How about a discussion of women suffrage or the Equal Rights Amendment or even income comparisons, since these subjects might allow women to feel distressed because they could view themselves as inferior to men?

A friend reminded me that these consequences might not be unintended. It might be a direct effort at controlling the content of curriculum that is destructive of a well-rounded education designed to promote critical thinking and analysis in favor of "feel good" classes that make people happy and thereby giving them a false sense of security. Indeed, the definition of a liberal arts education is a curriculum that generally includes language, chemistry, biology, geography, art, music, history, philosophy, civics, social sciences, and foreign languages. These subjects, as well as others, lie at the heart of education's purpose in preparing students for a productive life in a dynamic society by developing skills that maximize creativity and interpersonal skills. Additionally, education instills a sense of social responsibility which influences success in life, work and citizenship. The ability to analyze and engage in critical thinking is essential for the development of the mind. We know that uninformed disengaged citizens lead to poor policy choices that adversely impact life, work and citizenship.

This proposed legislation targets history, civics and social sciences, and strikes at the core of the purpose of a well-rounded education.

The Republicans have been very effective in flipping scripts, taking words such as "freedom," "liberty," "justice," etc., and attaching them to proposals and actions that are anti-Democratic and anti-freedom, anti-liberty, anti-justice, etc. In fact, this anti-history CRT proposal is called the "Individual Freedom" law. You can readily see how easy it is to flip the script.

But the Republican script of giving draconian laws calming, pleasant descriptions can be flipped by applying the law to actual unintended consequences—for the Republican Party.

And it's really quite simple. If CRT becomes the vehicle for re-writing the history of the civil rights movement in America, Black students might well feel psychologically distressed over this. Similarly, if watering down or re-writing the history of the Holocaust, genocide, ethnic cleansing, women's suffrage, etc., this could justifiably make affected particular groups "feel discomfort, guilt, anguish," etc., which would in turn give them the same rights to challenge the re-worked curriculum as it would those who oppose CRT and the other subjects as well.

So, a word to our esteemed Legislature: be careful what you wish for.

FLORIDA REPUBLICANS: "WHAT DAMAGE CAN WE DO TODAY?"

For today's episode of "What damage can we do today?" the Republican-controlled legislature is considering a bill backed by major state businesses that would ban local governments from setting wages at a rate higher than the state's minimum wage of $10 an hour.

Supporters in the legislature say allowing local wages to exceed the state's minimum stifles competition, undermines market forces, and increases costs for taxpayers. They believe that market forces should be the determinant of local minimum wages.

Although history is now a subject among Republicans that must not be taught truthfully lest it give them "psychological distress," perhaps some decent soul will remind them of where free market forces took our nation almost 100 years ago. Just invite these legislators to Google laissez fair, free enterprise, 1929, Great Depression.

https://www.tallahassee.com/story/news/politics/2022/01/26/florida-local-minimum-wages-would-gone-under-proposed-legislation/6611647001/

PROVE IT!

During the past couple of weeks, the Republican-led Florida Legislature considered two major pieces of legislation, but whether they actually accomplish what the legislature intended may well be another story.

The first targets Critical Race Theory teaching (but covers much more) by prohibiting individuals from making people "feel discomfort, guilt, anguish, or any other form of psychological distress on account of his or her race, color, sex, or national origin."

The second is a measure that would give businesses a right to sue when a local ordinance hurts their bottom line. The measure would create a cause of action for businesses if a local ordinance or charter amendment reduces the business' revenue or profits by 15%.

But whether the legislature considered what a person claiming psychological distress, or a business owner claiming a local law hurts his/her business, must go through and prove to win a lawsuit, is quite another matter.

PSYCHOLOGICAL DISTRESS--You see, to state a cause of action for intentional infliction of emotional distress (there doesn't appear to be a specific cause of action for psychological distress), a lawsuit must set out four elements: (1) deliberate or reckless infliction of mental suffering; (2) outrageous conduct; (3) the conduct caused the emotional distress; and (4) the distress was severe. Florida follows the physical impact rule (or Florida impact rule). This requires plaintiffs who want money for emotional distress to prove they also experienced some physical impact or that their emotional injuries somehow impacted them physically.

Consider what a plaintiff will face when filing a lawsuit for psychological distress: the person sued will hire a lawyer who will immediately seek discovery by, seeking all of plaintiff's medical records, going back months or perhaps years. Plaintiff's doctors will be compelled to provide all records, including notes, physical and mental exams, prescription records, etc. The person sued will want to see if the plaintiff is a chronic complainer, a malingerer, or a frivolous litigator. The person claiming distress will have to face being deposed under oath. Additionally, family members and friends may also be deposed to see if they can shed light on plaintiff's claims. The plaintiff will soon learn that discovery means just that.

And the plaintiff will have to prove his/her case by a preponderance of the evidence; that it is more likely than not that the facts are as the plaintiff claims. The plaintiff bears the burden of proving that all of the legal elements were present.

LAWSUITS AGAINST LOCAL GOVERNMENT FOR BUSINESS LOSSES--A similar situation faces a business owner who files a lawsuit against local government claiming an ordinance hurts his/her business. These types of cases are fact-intensive and generally require the business owner to carefully and fully document over a period of months, at least, by presenting

1. general ledgers or receipts.
2. spreadsheets.

3. income and expense journals (include a statement explaining why the claimed expenses relate to the business income).
4. travel log or mileage statement, if applicable.
5. Any other document or record that establishes business loss solely attributable to a local law.

Again, there is the discovery phase of the lawsuit. It is expected that the lawyer for the business will want to examine every piece of paper that the plaintiff is relying on, and will search mightily to see if the claimed loss is a direct result of the law, or shoddy or incompetent business practices, or any other reason other than the local law. A business owner can expect to be deposed under oath, and have his/her staff deposed as well. And, again, the owner will have to prove the case by a preponderance of the evidence.

It should be obvious that anyone suing under these proposals, assuming they become law, will have an uphill fight and, to wage it, will have to disclose things he or she might not want to be made known to the public.

CHUTZPAH! THE REPUBLICANS HAVE IT IN SPADES

Chutzpah is becoming more fashionably used these days to describe behavior. It is a Hebrew word, pronounced "hootspah" that means audacity, arrogance, gall, effrontery, temerity, nerve, or extreme self-confidence. However, because of its unique sound, it is becoming rather popular in our culture. Trying saying it loud. Notice the sound in your throat. That guttural sound is most appropriate. The word is used as a pejorative, expressing contempt or disapproval.

It takes chutzpah to:

1. Call those who attacked our Capitol on January 6 of last year patriots;
2. Cast a presidential election as "rigged" despite all the evidence to the contrary;
3. Restrict voting access to certain groups over others, based on historic voter patterns, in the name of preventing non-existent voter fraud;
4. Tamp down on academic freedom in the name of liberty and freedom;
5. Control school curriculum by eliminating studies that cause "psychological distress" or make people feel guilty, in the name of individual freedom;
6. Allow the state to trample upon local government home rule by controlling what ordinances local officials can pass, yet scream bloody murder when the federal government tries to assert the same control over the state;
7. Rely on hollow claims of "witch hunt" and "hoax" every time something takes place that draws some folks closer to the criminal justice system;
8. Brand any inquiry as "partisan" even though both parties are represented;

9. Allow businesses to sue local government over ordinances that they claim adversely affect their businesses, while claiming support for local government; and

10. Seek moral or functional equivalency to make some folks "feel good" whenever their mindset is challenged or they feel "psychological distress" of discomfort, when there is no legitimate basis for an equivalency claim.

These are just a few examples of behavior that can best be described as chutzpah. There are certainly others. Try it. The next time you see or hear something that stirs your interest, see if chutzpah is an apt description. These days, they happen all too frequently.

A CONSTITUTIONAL CONVENTION? IT CAN'T HAPPEN HERE! THINK AGAIN.

A few days ago, I posted some comments about how our Constitution could be changed—in fact, it can be re-written--to provide for an authoritarian takeover of the presidency. All that is required is that 38 state legislatures be in Republican hands.

But should 34 states call for a constitutional convention, far more sinister things can be done that could dramatically alter the face of our government going forward.

The United States Constitution provides for two ways that an amendment may be proposed: (1) either by a two-thirds vote of both Houses of Congress, or (2) by a convention called for that purpose if two-thirds of the 50 states request one. The amendment must then be ratified by three-fourths of the state legislatures, or three-fourths of conventions called in each state for ratification. Thus, changing the United States Constitution can be accomplished by 38 states without any congressional involvement.

Two-thirds of 50 is 34; three-fourths of 50 is 38. Currently, 30 state legislatures are controlled by Republicans; three are split. To achieve both levels, Republicans only need to add a few more states. Since a constitutional convention called by the states to change the constitution has never happened, and there are no rules or standards in place regarding how this process is to go forward, or what can be covered, it would be entirely up to the convention to decide what the constitution would look like.

Recently, Nebraska became the 17th state to call for a constitutional convention. While there are three subjects included in this call, two of which are vague, there is no limit on what subjects can be covered via the convention process. From the article posted below, it's not hard to imagine the chaos that could arise from such a convention.

Considering the times we live in, pay careful attention to what your state legislature is doing about calling for a constitutional convention. Our Democracy could well be on the line.

RECENT POLL SHOWS 72% OF AMERICANS THINK THE COUNTRY IS HEADED IN THE WRONG DIRECTION

The obvious question is what is the cause of this division. Is it:

1. Efforts to overturn the presidential election?
2. The press as "the enemy of the people?"
3. Too much academic freedom on our college and university campuses?
4. Teaching too much history or other subjects, making some people feel uncomfortable?
5. Too many books that shouldn't be read, justifying book banning?
6. Not enough access to guns under the Second Amendment to protect us?
7. Rallies by Neo-Nazi groups?
8. Bomb threats at HBCUs?
9. Attacks on law enforcement officers?
10. Investigations that are partisan, hoaxes, witch hunts?
11. Inaction by Congress on important issues?
12. Lack of leadership at the local, state and federal levels?
13. Lack of confidence in our executive, legislative and judicial branches of government?

14. A belief that our politicians are stoking the flames of anger and resentment, instead of being calming, reassuring influences?
15. A belief that we would be better off with a different form of government?
16. Rhetoric that has made hate fashionable or justifiable?

Is it all of the above? Are there possible causes omitted from this list? Is there a difference between causes and symptoms?

If three-fourths of the country is unhappy with how things are going, we need a strong reality check to get us on the right track internally, and we need this yesterday. There are international forces from the west and east that would relish a weakened, disillusioned America. We must be strong enough, and united enough, to deal with external threats. We need a search for solutions, and this must start with our elected officials. They are the ones directly accountable to us.

WHY I AM A DEMOCRAT

Recently, I had a discussion with a friend who's a died-in-the-wool conservative. During our conversation, I asked him why he is a conservative. He waxed about the Democrats giving handouts to those who didn't work for them; the drift of the country toward Socialism; and his support for limited government, less taxes and more freedom. In other words, he uttered the same refrain I've heard time and time again whenever the question arose.

Then, he asked me why I am a Democrat. I told him the story that was handed down to me by my grandfather and father. Here it is.

My grandfather, who never got beyond high school, was a jeweler in New York City. He was a very successful jeweler, making rings for people of prominence. (In fact, today I proudly wear the ring he made for me when I was a teenager, and the ring he made for my dad which became mine when he passed away in 1988. These rings are one-of-kind gold and diamond initial rings. Although my dad and I have the same first and last name, I am not named after him; I'm named after my great-grandfather. Hence, my middle name Lee.)

When the Great Depression hit in 1929, my grandfather lost much of his fortune. Times were tough; my dad was 20 and my uncle was 16. Grandpa had to provide for his family, and he struggled.

But a few of his patrons were influential people, and they used their connections to have the governor of New York appoint my grandfather clerk of the Bronx County Jail. This clerkship was equivalent to a clerk of court; handling all administrative matters for this large county jail. He served in this position for a couple of years, which allowed him to get back on his feet financially and resume his career as a jeweler. I still have his badge in its original leather case. It's over 90 years old.

And the governor who appointed my grandfather and saved him from financial ruination—Franklin Delano Roosevelt.

And that's why I'm a Democrat.

BACK TO THE DARK AGES

This makes me both sad and angry. Sad that we've come to this point at a time when we should be celebrating our greatest enlightenment. History should have taught us to avoid what has befallen our ancestors. Angry that the better angels in us have allowed this to happen. My greatest fear is the closing off of avenues of learning. Banning books and prohibiting certain studies are classic ways of dumbing down a society. And without learning, it is impossible to know.

There is no Holocaust for those who don't know about it. There is no racial discrimination if people aren't informed about its history. If the facts of zoning patterns are taught to show how race has impacted living conditions, this isn't Critical Race Theory, unless someone successfully claims it is before an uniformed judiciary. I recall a most direct statement from former Harvard President Derek Bok--"If you think education is expensive, try ignorance."

ANOTHER ATTACK ON "THE ENEMY OF THE PEOPLE"

After the Supreme Court takes care of abortion by either reversing Roe v. Wade, or limiting it to the point where it has virtually no significance, the Court will set its sights on the current status of defamation law as it applies to public officials and public figures.

The current standard for proving defamation or libel under New York Times v. Sullivan, is that a public official or public figure must prove actual malice; that is, that the challenged statement was made with "knowledge that it was false or with reckless disregard of whether it was false or not."

Two Supreme Court justices recently challenged the constitutional propriety of this standard, saying it isn't grounded in the constitution as understood by our founding fathers. (Of course, this is the same argument that was made by those who want to invalidate Roe v. Wade.)

Just the other day, a judge on Florida's First District Court of Appeal followed these two justices, noting that the current standard for proving actual malice against the media in particular is far too high. (Overlooked in his analysis was the fact that cases have been won under this actual malice standard. If the media knew a statement was false, or did absolutely nothing to verify its untruthfulness, how hard is that to prove?)

Not to be outdone, Sarah Palin currently is litigating a libel claim against the New York Times, not to win in the federal district court which is required to follow Times v. Sullivan, but to get her case to the Supreme Court where she is hoping the six conservative justices will do to Times v. Sullivan what they are expected to do to Roe v. Wade.

Unanswered in the conservatives' opposition to the Times case is what standard they would substitute for actual malice. The Florida judge noted three media considerations; investigation, fact-checking and editing. But that doesn't address the specific standard of proof for a public officer or person to successfully make out a defamation claim.

If, for example, a newspaper talks to three sources and gets the same story, using the same or similar words, and that information is reported, but it's found to be false, and that in hindsight, perhaps the reporter should have spoken to a fourth or fifth person, is this the standard the judges are talking about? In short, if the reporter in fact investigated, checked facts and the story was edited, would that be enough to overcome a defamation lawsuit? Recognizing that journalism is literature in a hurry, and that the value of the news is getting it to the public as quickly and as accurately as possible, would the Supreme Court impose a standard on the mass media that adversely impacts their ability to report consistent with the First Amendment's call that" debate on public issues should be uninhibited, robust, and wide-open."

How would the elimination of the Times standard of actual malice affect this "uninhibited, robust, and wide-open" debate on public issues by public officials and public persons?

Would the Court impose a "reasonable man" standard, requiring a reporter to show that what he or she did was what a reasonable reporter would do under the circumstances of time and the importance of robust, uninhibited reporting?

We know that public officials are held to a high standard; after all, a public office is a public trust. And part of that high standard is to be able to stand the heat; remember Harry Truman's admonition: "If you can't stand the heat, get out of the kitchen." Or words to that effect.

Public figures likewise have for the most part sought the limelight; shouldn't they be held to a higher standard, since so many tend to identify with a famous actor, singer, etc.? Don't public figures have an obligation to the emulating public and the limelight they actively sought?

If the Supreme Court ultimately decides to trash Times v. Sullivan, and allows public officials and public figures to be treated like everyone else, it should be self-evident what the effect will be on a vigorous press protected by the First Amendment. The press will be timid in its reporting; facts the public should know most likely will never the light of day. If chilling the press in its First Amendment obligation is the goal; if tamping down debate on issues of public importance is the goal; they will be accomplished by eliminating the Times standard.

WHAT DOES "LEGISLATING FROM THE BENCH" REALLY MEAN?

I have never heard the phrase "legislating from the bench" used by someone who supports the particular decision. It's used by those who oppose a particular ruling. But judges do legislate from the bench, particularly when deciding constitutional issues. Nowhere in the Constitution is due process, equal protection, privileges and immunities, etc. defined. So judges have to define them.

There are two schools of thought here. Originalists look to what the words meant when drafted; living constitutionalists apply those words to current conditions. Each side says the other is wrong; yet the Constitution itself is silent as to what interpretive standard is to be used. Roe v. Wade was founded on privacy considerations set out in the Constitution, yet expanded to cover current conditions. You know, the right to be secure in our persons and effects. Times v. Sullivan was founded on the "public office is a public trust" and "uninhibited, robust debate" principles. Neither is set out in the Constitution; yet the Court used other guideposts to reach its conclusion. Some would argue that Bush v. Gore constituted legislating from the bench. The debate over what standard is to be used in interpreting the Constitution will no doubt continue. But what constitutes legislating from the bench is, in the final analysis, in the eye of the beholder. Makes for interesting discussions, though.

Legislators would pass a law in a heartbeat if they could require all news reports to be of a positive nature. Officials would love that free positive publicity. It's no surprise that defamation lawsuits are filed only when a report is negative. But, of course, a defamation suit itself generates publicity, and there are times when that's all a public official wants.

There are, however, instances of successful lawsuits under the Times standard. Sure, the standard is high; proof must be by clear and convincing evidence. Still, it's not an impossible burden. I think the Court will try to devise a standard that is a middle ground between the Times and lawsuits against private persons. Perhaps proof by a preponderance of the evidence that the story didn't meet the investigative, fact-gathering and editing standards of what a reasonable reporter/news medium would do under the circumstances, against the backdrop of the pressure of time and the First Amendment's charge of robust reporting. But then again, doesn't this, too, smack of legislating from the bench?

Here's a great story about Justice Scalia. He was on a program debating Justice Breyer. During a Q and A, Scalia was asked about an opinion he wrote that didn't square with his originalist approach. Scalia is reported to have said "It's not my burden to prove originalism is perfect," adding that it was his job to prove it was the better approach. The latter part of his statement is, of course, subject to endless debate. I doubt we'll ever see the day when one approach to constitutional interpretation is forever favored over the other.

THE SECOND "BIG LIE"

For the past 15 months, we have been regaled with the original "Big Lie" of a "rigged election" that former President Trump and his band of acolytes and diehards have repeated over and over again, ad infinitum ad nauseam. This is part of an historical playbook in which a lie repeated often enough, can become the truth, at least for far too many people.

Now, we have the "Second Big Lie," this one put forth by the Republican National Committee in censuring Reps. Liz Cheney and Adam Kitzinger for their work on the House committee investigating the January 6 attack on our nation's capital. These two representatives were called out by the RNC for "participating in a Democrat-led persecution of ordinary citizens engaged in legitimate political discourse."

This is history repeating itself again, only this time it's the history of repeating a lie often enough, and enough people will accept it as the truth. The Republican Party is now on record asking Americans to ignore their eyes and ears and simply believe the incredible claim that all that happened on that infamous January 6 was nothing more than "ordinary citizens engaged in legitimate political discourse." Remember, these are the same folks who attacked Black Lives Matter and Antifa for rioting during racial protests.

That quote from the RNC will no doubt have a special place in historic infamy as clearly and graphically showing the true colors of the current version of the Republican Party. It is now a party that no longer prides itself on Democratic principles or even our constitutional form of government. It is now the party of authoritarianism with a win-at-all-cost-mentality; a classic end justifies the means approach to governance. For them, it's not about policy as much as it is about power—power to do whatever they want whenever they want, Democracy be damned.

Let's break down this infamous quote into three parts.

"PARTICIPATING IN A DEMOCRAT-LED PERSECUTION"

These two representatives were appointed to the investigating committee after House Republican leader Kevin McCarthy blocked any party member from serving on it.

Remember, this is the party that champions individual accountability and personal responsibility. Yet, the party leadership clearly wants no part of unearthing the truth behind the attack that came perilously close to a takeover of our national government. The Republicans want to protect Donald Trump and those who aided and abetted their attempted coup, and will block any inquiry into the truth behind this seditious attack. Those who engaged in criminal activity are not being persecuted; they're being charged with violating the law—consistent with the Republican Party's claim that it is the party of law and order.

"ORDINARY CITIZENS"

Those who attacked the Capitol were hardly "ordinary citizens." They were White Supremacists, Neo-Nazis and their sympathizers and supporters who, stoked by flaming rhetoric from Trump and his sycophants, marched to the Capitol with one purpose in mind: to prevent the duly elected president from taking office and having Trump declared the winner.

"LEGITIMATE POLITICAL DISCOURSE"

The party of law and order evidently doesn't apply that tagline to the criminal conduct of its backers. That the party leadership would make such a claim shows a lack of decency and compassion for those who were carrying out their official duties and were brutally assaulted for their efforts. The party's claim of "legitimate political discourse" would be laughable if it didn't come from what one would expect to be a reputable source. But, as we all know, some will sell their souls rather than seek the truth. in legitimate p

But this committee will unearth the truth, and its report will show that. This is precisely what the Republicans fear. And the only way to avoid this is to make noise about partisanship. They realize that if Trump survived two impeachments and avoided a third following the issuance of the Mueller Report, all they have to do is double down with enough noise that will convince enough people to believe the committee report is nothing more than political theater.

The Republicans hope enough people won't dig into that report to find out that Trump and other party faithful organized, prosecuted, aided and abetted an attempt to trump the constitutional process of certifying a presidential election and illegally install the losing candidate into office. So far, the scope and depth of this conspiracy is coming out in slow drips. Soon, it will all be put together in a carefully constructed hour-by-hour, day-by-day chronology. No matter how hard the Republicans try to bury the truth, it does have a stubborn way of coming out. Then, it will be up to the rest of us to do what must be done to assure the continuation of our Democracy.

HOW DO WE BREAK THROUGH THE WALL?

There are millions out there who firmly believe that:

1. Donald Trump won the 2020 presidential election.
2. Joe Biden is an illegitimate president.
3. Mike Pence is a traitor.
4. Those who attacked the Capitol were engaging in "legitimate political discourse."
5. The press is "the enemy of the people."
6. There are nice Neo-Nazis and White Supremacists.

7. Books of their choosing must be banned.
8. The history of race relations can't be taught if it makes some people feel uncomfortable.
9. Fair elections weren't fair, and therefore election laws must be changed.
10. Academic freedom means not upsetting political leaders with opposition commentary.

I could go on and on listing outrageous, factually vacuous, logically twisted beliefs held by millions, and it seems this list continues to grow just about every day.

Those of us who take the time to post articles and personal thoughts on Facebook over the past few years are, unfortunately, preaching to the choir. We ask ourselves how can it be that millions of hard-working people harbor such beliefs; some so strongly or so easily swayed that they would dare attack the greatest symbols of our Democracy— our Capitol and the sanctity of the ballot?

And how can these people change their mind when they fervently believe those who don't agree with them are wrongheaded, uneducated and can't see the Socialist forest through the Communist trees? Are they so focused on the fear of Socialism that they are willing to accept any form of authoritarianism? When they call Democrats Fascists or Nazis, how do you persuade them otherwise?

There are scientific studies that deal with people who hold such strong beliefs, and we know that if stoked by elected and appointed leaders, these beliefs become acceptable and fashionable enough to be publicly displayed.

But back to my question. How do we break through that wall that allows for such anti-Democratic thinking that defies fact, logic, and reason? These believers attended the same schools, work, worship, shop and attend functions with the rest of us.

Perhaps instead of posting the latest example that defies reality, we should instead focus on how we can deal with what is to us lunacy or worse?

A solution is way above my pay grade, but perhaps collectively we can start a dialogue that reaches a common ground founded on fact, logic, common sense, and reality, along with understanding and compassion. Perhaps I'm too idealistic, but one thing is certain: we can't maintain the status quo.

WE KNOW WHAT THEY STAND FOR; WHAT'S NEXT?

Does anyone out there have any doubt what the loud, shrill voices that purport to represent the leadership of the Republican Party stand for, and where they want to take the country? It's not as if their agenda is hidden; rather, it's out there for all to see.

When they re-write history, such as calling the January 6 attack on the Capitol "legitimate political discourse," do you believe this? When they declare that academic freedom applies only when it supports the Republicans in power; when they tear up curriculum by banning discussions on race, ethnicity, gender or any other related subject that might cause discomfort by being exposed to the truth; when they authorize citizens to sue each other, does this bother you?

When they declare they are the law-and-order party, but are deaf and blind to the crimes committed by their own, do you find this disturbing? Or are you so focused on their cries of socialism and communism that you fail to see, or ignore, the fascism openly on display in their rhetoric and actions?

It seems only the ignorant or indifferent fail to see where the Republican Party is taking the country. For them, democracy no longer works. So, they have to adjust the playing field by upending the right to vote. They are well aware of historic voting patterns; this is why, in the name of protecting against voting fraud—which does not exist in any wide fashion and for which the Republican Party has offered no evidence to convince any court in the country to the contrary—they have doubled down on restricting certain groups from exercising their constitutional right to vote. And yes, the right to vote is in our Constitution; see Amendments 15, 19, 24 and 26.

While they scream about federal government interference with "state's rights," they have no difficulty clamping down on local governments, again allowing citizens to sue local governments—local home rule be damned. The sole purpose of this effort is to control local government.

For the Republican Party, it's not about leadership; it's about control. Go through your history; recall the major legislative achievements of the New Deal in the 1930s that helped lift us out of the Great Depression: 1. Emergency Banking Relief Act (1933); 2. Civilian Conservation Corps (1933); 3. Agricultural Adjustment Act (1933); 4. Tennessee Valley Authority Act (1933) 5. National Industrial Recovery Act (1933); 6. Public Works Administration (1933); 7. Securities Exchange Act (1934); 8. National Housing Act (1934); 9. Works Progress Administration (1935); 10. National Labor Relations Act (1935); 11. Social Security Act (1935); 12. Fair Labor Standards Act (1938).

Fast forward to the mid-1960s when the Civil Rights and Voting Rights acts were passed, along with Medicare and Medicaid.

Now ask yourself which party had the White House as well as a majority in Congress when all of these bills passed. Certainly, Republicans helped, but these laws were not the stuff of Republican Party leadership.

I have repeatedly asked for the identity of a single piece of major legislation that passed by a Republican-led Congress and signed by a Republican president that benefitted the most people in our country; more, if possible. I'm still waiting.

There are those who place the blame for our current state of affairs on Donald Trump. I tend to disagree. I think the seeds of hatred, divisiveness, anger, etc., have always been there. He just gave vent to certain forces that allowed them to believe their rhetoric is fashionable; and too many politicians, seeing an opportunity born of resentment, decided to ride the wave by further fanning the flames with heated rhetoric.

So, where do we go from here? First, those who broke the law must be prosecuted to the fullest extent of the law. This includes those in high public office. Claims of partisanship, witch hunt, etc., are as old as the hills and screamed the loudest by those trying to gain cover for themselves. Don't fall prey to that nonsense. We have a criminal justice system that has been tested since our nation's founding, and history has proven it to be the best system ever devised to ascertain the truth. Don't let the naysayers and the deniers of truth lead you astray.

Second, cooler heads and better angels must come forward and in unmistakable terms tell the shrill voices that enough is enough. And it must start by taking to task those politicians who have the unmitigated gall to foment lies, support fake science, give out deliberate misinformation, and who generally commit malfeasance, misfeasance, and other conduct beneath the dignity of their office. A breach of their oath justifies removal from office. Public office is, and must always be, a public trust. No one has a right to public office.

When they scream their usual mindless rhetoric, they must immediately be called out. To those who choose to remain in the party but who refuse to buy into the madness that has engulfed too many in leadership positions, they must be on the front line of demonstrating moral rectitude and a strong backbone, and take back their party. Tepid, one-time responses aren't enough.

To be sure, this is a Republican Party problem, and some sanity is beginning to emerge within, especially from those who originally bought into some of the harsh, false rhetoric. But with our time-tested institutions and guardrails on the line, fact, reason, logic, common sense and critical thinking must carry the day. There really is no other choice.

NOT A GOOD DAY FOR DESANTIS, TRUMP

The top two Republicans didn't have a good day yesterday.

DeSantis

The Florida Supreme Court refused to give cover to DeSantis's efforts to undermine Rep. Al Lawson's congressional district, among others, by declining to answer the governor's questions about requirements for congressional redistricting. Because this type of redistricting is accomplished in the same manner as the passage of any piece of legislation—a bill passed by the legislature and signed by the governor—essentially what DeSantis was asking the Court to do is to tell him what his duties are as applied to any legislation. This, of course, would open up the Court to answering a governor's question just about every time he has to consider signing a bill into law. The Court deftly avoided this slippery slope by declaring that the use of this advisory opinion tool in a governor's arsenal addresses only rare and little used situations. Pointedly, the justices appointed by DeSantis joined in the unanimous decision.

Trump

Donald Trump's latest problem is potentially far more onerous. Remember how he railed against Hillary Clinton for misuse of her email account? Remember how the Republicans joined him in lockstep outrage over what they said was the biggest scandal since Watergate? Well, it seems our immediate past president was seen by several folks flushing torn up documents down a White House toilet. (As an aside, there has to be some irony here, or perhaps a metaphor, for a president standing over a commode watching flushed pieces of public presidential records going round and round, down and out. No doubt he and his cronies will call this latest episode just a bunch of crap.)

Destroying public records isn't a good thing. So, rather typical of him, Trump has denied doing any such thing, even though it's pretty clear several saw him do it, or knew he did it from others who did observe the serial flushing. So, who are you going to believe, those who say they saw him flush away, or Donald Trump? Well, we know Trump's penchant for telling the truth, and we also know he will never appear in any forum under oath. And we know why. Something about testifying falsely under oath on a matter of material importance. It's called perjury.

While proof of a violation of public records laws would be relatively easy if several eyewitnesses to Flushingate testify, the laws are somewhat murky as far as liability is concerned. The president does have certain powers over classified documents, and then there's that provision in the Constitution about the president having to "take Care that the Laws be faithfully executed" which some scholars say applies to his duties as to other agencies, not specifically to a president's duties regarding his records. (I can't help but note another irony here. Nixon had Watergate; Trump now has Flushingate; what is it about water that ties these two presidents together? Perhaps it's the fact that people can drown in water.)

Still, if several testify as to their personal knowledge of Trump destroying presidential records, or secreting classified records at his palace in Mar-A-Lago, Trump has a problem. If he doesn't testify, it's their word and there's alone. If he does testify, he opens himself up to all sorts of things, nothing that's helpful to him, especially after his attacks on Hillary Clinton.

But all things considered, this latest scandal hitting Trump may be the least of his worries.

No, not a good day at all for the top two.

CHANGING THE CONSTITUTION WITHOUT CHANGING A WORD

Typically, whenever a law is passed that arouses strong anger or resentment, those who oppose it inevitably utter these words: IT'S UNCONSTITUTIONAL!!

No doubt, considering current dynamics, this utterance is appearing quite frequently these days.

Whether it be legislation affecting voting rights, critical race theory (whatever that might be), free speech, abortion, open carry guns, academic freedom, peaceful protests, gerrymandering of legislative districts, employer-employee relations, national health care, and on and on, if it's a hot-button social or political issues, you can bet that opponents will shout IT'S UNCONSTITUTIONAL as they march into court.

To be sure, they may well be right insofar as constitutional law is currently understood. But suppose what is guaranteed or protected today by the constitution becomes illegal tomorrow?

The United States Supreme Court is the final arbiter of what the United States Constitution means. The Supreme Court said this 219 years ago. (The Florida Supreme Court is the final arbiter of the state constitution and laws of Florida, and its decisions are binding authority for all other Florida state courts and for federal courts when they apply Florida law. In most instances, the only appeal from the Florida Supreme Court is to the U.S. Supreme Court on questions of federal law.)

When a law is passed and its constitutionality is considered, this is initially done through the lens of the constitution as it is currently understood, based on existing case law, or precedent. But while the Supreme Court gives great deference to precedent, especially long-standing case law, there is nothing in the constitution itself that tells the Court how the justices must interpret it, or what deference is to be accorded current case law, or what principles they must apply in determining the constitutionality of a law. All of the principles, standards and tests for determining the constitutionality of a law are made by the justices themselves. Every one of them.

To be sure, there are those who believe it takes a lot of effort to amend the constitution, and therefore any concern about the constitution changing meanings literally overnight is engaging in alarmist tactics.

Not true.

Currently, before the United States Supreme Court, there is a case that could well signal the death knell of abortion rights in the country; efforts to overturn Roe v. Wade. There are also cases wending their way through the federal judiciary questioning the constitutionality of the previously validated federal Voting Rights Act, as well as ways to make it easier for public officials and public figures to sue the news media for defamation. Then there's the question of whether the Second Amendment allows for open carry of firearms on our public streets. No doubt there will be other cases dealing with the scope of peaceful protests, voting rights, free speech, academic freedom, business v. labor issues, and on and on.

How can constitutional law be changed so that what the constitution means today might well be the opposite of what it means tomorrow?

It's really quite simple. There are nine justices on the United States Supreme Court. It takes five for a majority to declare what the constitution means. Remember, the Court is the final arbiter of what our sacred document means. (For the Florida Supreme Court, it takes a majority of four to decide what the state constitution means.)

That's it. Get five justices to agree at the federal level, and what the Unites States Constitution means today most certainly could be different from what it meant yesterday. **It's not the words of the constitution that have changed; rather, it's the interpretation placed on those words**

by the Court's majority. And if you think this is a rare occurrence, think again. According to the Congressional Research Service, the United States Supreme

Court has overruled itself on constitutional cases over 140 times, yet not a single word in the constitution was changed.

Make no mistake about it, when Mitch McConnell and his cohorts fought so hard to get conservative justices on the Court, his goal was and is to change what the constitution means, at least on those hot-button issues that conservatives believe are anathema to their ideological beliefs.

As these issues make their way through Congress (and state legislatures) and finally into the courts, it's important to pay attention, and to understand the dynamics of appointments to the highest court in our nation. After all, their decisions affect your life.

A WORD ABOUT TREASON

As news circulates of Hillary Clinton allegedly spying on Donald Trump to see if the Russians aided his campaign, Trump predictably called this worse than Watergate, and his most rabid supporters are screaming "treason."

They also accused Clinton of treason for her sloppy handling of her government email account back in 2016. Pointedly, although both houses of Congress, and the White House, were in Republican hands from 2017 to 2019—and with control over all of the 93 federal prosecutors' offices---not a single charge was ever brought against Clinton in connection with her email. Why? Because even Trump's most ardent supporters knew they could never prove a violation of federal law.

Yet, to this day, now fueled by this latest report, there is still the widely held belief by the most rabid of Trump supporters that Clinton committed treason. As a result, it's important to look at how federal law defines treason. The Constitution, Article III, Section 3, Clause 1, provides that:

"Treason against the United States, shall consist only in levying War against them, or in adhering to their Enemies, giving them Aid and Comfort. No Person shall be convicted of Treason unless on the testimony of two Witnesses to the same overt Act, or on Confession in open Court."

Let's take the two allegations against Clinton. First, the misuse of her email account.

Did her conduct constitute levying war against the United States? Did it constitute giving aid and comfort to our nation's enemies? No on both accounts. If it were any other way, you can bet with Republican control over two branches of our federal government, charges would have been filed.

Second, spying on the Trump campaign and the White House. Assuming this is true, does this constitute levying war against the United States? Or does this give aid and comfort to the enemy? No on both accounts here. Again, assuming this allegation is true, its purpose was to determine whether the Trump campaign was being aided and abetted by the Russians. This is hardly waging war against America, or giving aid and comfort to the enemy. Actually, it's the reverse; Clinton was attempting to see whether the Trump campaign received aid and comfort from Russia.

This may come as a shock to some, but candidate spying on an opponent's campaign is nothing new. We know longtime FBI Director J. Edgar Hoover had multiple files on politicians and made certain information known to preferred candidates.

Among politicians, however, it's not called spying. It's called opposition research, and it involves gathering information from multiple sources that paint the opposing candidate in a negative light. This also includes embedding supporters in opponent's campaigns by attending rallies, making friends with opposition supporters, and on and on. Opposition research is legal, so long as surveillance devices and techniques that are barred by law are not employed.

Now, let's apply the definition of treason to Trump's conduct that resulted in two impeachments.

First, Trump's phone call with the Ukrainian president seeking information on Joe Biden's son, Hunter, to help in Trump's re-election campaign. Again, did this phone call constitute levying war against America? Did it give our enemies aid and comfort? No on both counts. Whatever this phone call is when placed against other federal criminal laws, treason isn't one of them.

Second, the January 6 attack on the Capitol. Did Trump's actions constitute levying war against the United States? Did it give aid and comfort to the enemy? These are tougher calls, because the purpose of the assault was to stop the constitutional process of finally selecting the next president and vice president of the United States. But did that assault constitute an act of war, or materially aid our enemies? We most likely will never find out, because that assault—both its lead up and its aftermath—are governed by other federal laws.

How about destroying presidential and other public records? While not an act of war, does this provide aid and comfort to our enemies? I suppose this depends on what was destroyed. We'll have to wait and see on this one.

An important point here is that if folks are going to toss around the serious criminal charge of treason, it's a good idea to know what they're talking about. Clearly, those who in the past, and again now, accuse Clinton of treason don't know what they're talking about. Whether it be through ignorance or indifference, they don't comprehend the definition of treason.

But their silence in the face of Trump's actions says a lot.

WHY DO STATES HAVE DIFFERENT LAWS, ESPECIALLY FOR THE SAME CONDUCT?

It certainly makes sense for each state to have its own laws, so long as they don't conflict with the federal constitution and laws. After all, each state has unique geography and natural resources, location, population demographics, historical operation of business, commerce and industry, community standards and public policies, etc. For example, oil and gas law is essential in some states, but certainly not in others.

It also makes sense for federal law to govern subjects that apply universally and should not be subject to a state-by-state approach, such as immigration, bankruptcy, patent and copyright, Social Security and SSI, federal anti-discrimination, and federal criminal laws.

It is these differences among the several states, however, that are cited in support of state laws regarding businesses, motor carriers, gambling, gun control, marriage, divorce, custody, certain criminal laws, and the like.

Then, there's abortion. Of course, it can be argued that community standards and public policy compel allowing each state to decide for itself what the law should be for abortion. But the fact is a woman's body is the same in every state. The period of gestation is the same for every woman (give or take a few days, it's going to be nine months, and there isn't anything that anyone can do about that).

So, if a woman is the same in all 50 states—and elsewhere around the world, for that matter—why is abortion to be treated on a state-by-state basis? Why should anything other than medical science and the doctor-patient relationship play any role? Why should certain groups dictate to others what they can or cannot do as it relates to abortion? Shouldn't abortion be about personal choice? And shouldn't these questions be addressed at the national level?

Some would make a similar argument about gun control. A gun is Wisconsin is as deadly as a gun in Florida. A bullet that injures or takes a life in Oregon is the same for Georgia. An assault rifle in one state is the same assault rifle in all the others. Because of the Second Amendment that applies nationwide, there is presumably even greater justification for uniform firearms laws that apply equally throughout the country.

Each state also has its own set of criminal laws, but the same question can be asked as noted above. Why do some states have the death penalty, while others don't? First degree premeditated murder is the same for all states; why isn't the penalty the same? Robbery in Texas is the same as in Connecticut. This can be equally said for just about every crime there is. So, why the difference depending on which state you're in?

History doesn't favor the expansion of nationalization of virtually all laws, however. After all, driving in a mountainous state imposes different conditions than driving in a state known for its flat lands. And the claim of state's rights and the Tenth Amendment still resonate loudly today.

But we also have a history of nationalizing laws to meet national crises; the Great Depression and the New Deal legislation of the 1930s, and civil and voting rights of the 1960s and most recent examples.

Nationalization of laws formally delegated to the states is nothing new or novel. Much of this depends on how the Constitution is interpreted. Those who favor the originalist or textualist approach will more likely support state laws that differ from one another. Those who support the "living document" approach will look to changing standards and public attitudes to justify nationalization efforts. Just examine the Warren Court's treatment of segregation and integration and expansion of criminal law and procedure during the period of 1953 to 1969.

Interestingly, it is those community standards and public policy claims that support both the state-by-state lawmaking under the Tenth Amendment and state's rights banner, and nationalization claims of the contemporaneous standards/ living document approach. There are indeed two sides to the same coin; it just depends on which side is relied upon.

Which, of course, means the debate between state's rights and nationalization will continue, because this fundamental issue lies at the heart of our representative Democracy and provides an answer to the ultimate question of what kind of nation we want to be.

WHY ARE CHALLENGES TO LEGISLATION FAVORED BY GOVERNOR DESANTIS BEING FILED IN FEDERAL COURT?

Thus far, several challenges to Republican Gov. Ron DeSantis's proposals passed by the Republican-led legislature have been filed in federal court. One reason for this is because those challenges implicate the federal constitution and federal laws.

But there is another underlying reason, and one that predicts that future challenges will wind up in federal courts, if the challengers have their way.

Take a look at the makeup of the Florida courts. All seven supreme court justices were appointed by Republican governors. All but three of the current 64 district court of appeal judges were appointed by Republican governors. And 396 trial court (circuit and county courts) were appointed by Republican governors.

Since the Republicans have controlled the executive and legislative branches of state governor for the past 23 years, and it is safe to assume that party will control both branches for years into the future, it is entirely realistic to believe that over the next few years, the vast majority, if not the entirety, of the judicial branch will consist of Republican judges. (Only trial judges stand for election under Florida's constitution; all appellate judges are selected through a commission nomination and voter retention system.

Therefore, it is reasonable to conclude that all of Florida's appellate judges will be appointed by Republican governors. Trial judges are still elected, but vacancies are filled by appointment. The number of initially elected trial judges is diminishing, and this trend can be expected to continue.)

Considering the composition of the Florida judiciary, it can easily be expected that those who challenge laws passed by Republican legislatures and signed by Republican governors will make every effort to cast their cases as a violation of federal law in order to get into federal court.

The only exception may be the legislative and congressional redistricting plans. Both plans must conform to Florida's constitutional Fair Districts amendments. If a challenge is predicated on these amendments, they will have to be litigated in state court because such a challenge is based on state, not federal, law. But there is also the impact of the federal Voting Rights Act, which could well lead to a federal lawsuit. However, over the past few years, the United States Supreme Court has been eroding the impact of this law. Therefore, how and where lawsuits will be filed remains to be seen.

But at least we know why challenges have been filed in federal courts, and why future challenging litigants will look to the federal courts for relief.

THE PERIL OF NON-ACCOUNTABILITY

Our entire judicial system is based on holding people accountable for their conduct. In civil law, a breach of a duty or obligation is met with a lawsuit designed to hold the violator accountable. In criminal law, an offense against a person or property subjects the offender to criminal penalties of imprisonment and/or fines in the name of the government whose duty it is (through the chief executive) to see that the law is faithfully executed. This has been our guiding star since the founding of our nation.

But every time Donald Trump is faced with accountability for his conduct, he typically rages that it's a witch hunt, a hit job, fake news, a partisan attack by radical left-wing Democrats, and on and on. He has his chorus of members of Congress, officials in state capitals, and millions of true believing Trumpites who echo his every word.

In their anger and rage, Congressional Republicans have made no secret that once they regain power, they will launch investigations on Democrats, empowered by a sense of self-righteousness that what's good for the goose is good for the gander. Recall that it was Sen. Ted Cruz who said a Republican Congress would move to impeach Joe Biden even if there was no justification for it, relying on the goose-gander analogy.

But what happens if, in a year from now, Biden is thrust into the same orbit now occupied by Trump?

Will Joe Biden call these investigations a witch hunt, a hit job, fake news, a partisan attack by radical right-wing authoritarians? And will his supporters in Congress, state capitals, and the millions who voted for him echo his every word?

Will Biden and his supporters avoid congressional subpoenas, subpoenas by federal or state prosecutors, appeal every action, take the Fifth Amendment, etc.? In short, will he be compelled to do exactly what his predecessor has done, and is doing?

The answer is we don't know, and won't know unless this dark scenario becomes reality. (Although, judging from past conduct, we have a fairly good idea how the Democrats will handle such an eventuality.)

But here's what we do know. What will suffer is the rule of law. If high public officials can avoid accountability, what does this say about the average citizen who is called upon to obey the law every day? If we can do what we want whenever we want with no accountability for our behavior, we no longer have an ordered society. Add to this sense of self-empowerment, an "I'm better than you" mentality, easier access to guns, and the fictional dystopian society we read about years ago becomes our sad reality.

And what affect would this scenario be on the need for national unity, especially in times of crisis? We know we are in competition with China, and Russia is flexing its might again. An enemy's greatest strength is the weakness of its opposition. The answer to this question should be obvious: as divided as we are now, that division will only widen and deepen.

To avoid this, there must be accountability for aberrant behavior. If there is probable cause to believe a crime has been committed, an investigation must ensue. If the investigation produces evidence of a crime, charges must be filed. Upon the filing of charges, our constitution and its jurisprudence assure the accused of a fair trial before an impartial factfinder. An adjudication of guilt allows for appeals. But once this process is completed, the results must be accepted.

Our nation simply can't tolerate or withstand a marked deviation from our judicial norms. We must avoid going down a rabbit hole from which we can't escape.

IRONIES OF IRONY

Recall that during the 2016 presidential campaign, Hillary Clinton handed Donald Trump a rallying cry that he used to stoke up the ire of his diehard supporters. Remember "Lock Her Up?"

Whenever he had the chance to remind his audience of her sloppy handling of her government email account, he would do so. And it helped Trump win the presidency.

But even though he had control of all of the nation's prosecuting attorneys, and both houses of Congress, from 2017 to 2019, not a single charge was ever filed against Clinton.

Just recently, it was reported that a special counsel concluded that the Clinton campaign spied both on Trump's campaign, and during his early years in the White House. Gleefully, Trump jumped on that bandwagon, saying what she did was worse than Watergate and the biggest scandal ever. (Trump is knows for hyperbole, to say the least.) Only this latest matter was found to be a nothingburger. This one-day news story is now history.

But with criminal investigations aimed at Trump, as well as some members of his family, his most ardent congressional supporters, and his White House staff, wouldn't it be the irony of ironies if it's not Hillary Clinton, but Donald Trump, who faces the reality of "Lock Him Up?"

We already know that his January 6 band of "peaceful protestors" who were "engaging in legitimate political discourse" according to the Republican National Committee, are either behind bars or awaiting trial, possible conviction and incarceration.

And with investigations ongoing in New York, Georgia, and in the House of Representatives, and possibly other places as well, the prospect of criminal charges being filed against Trump is not the product of idle speculation, wishful thinking, or the "it can't happen" true believers.

Already, House Republicans have promised that should they gain control of the House, they will stop the investigation in its tracks. The Democrats know this. This is why the House investigation will be completed on the committee's time schedule, with its final report issued well in advance of November. That report will be damning regardless of the lack of cooperation from many Republican operatives who, although they wax accountability and transparency, they mean this for you, not them.

Likewise, the New York investigation will be completed according to the prosecutor's timetable. That prosecutor happens to be a Democrat, and Trump has attacked the prosecutor using all sorts of epithets designed to undermine her efforts. The Georgia investigation will also be completed timely. In that probe, Trump has also seen fit to try to undermine its integrity by making ad hominem claims against the prosecutor. Making an enemy of a prosecutor in the hopes his minions will believe it's a witch hunt is not a smart move. Well, maybe it is with his base, but his base can't keep him from answering to criminal charges, and they certainly can't keep him from facing the penalties for committing crimes.

When Richard Nixon faced possible criminal charges in connection with Watergate, President Gerald Ford pardoned him. Since Trump was behind the move to indict Clinton for her email issues, he certainly wouldn't have pardoned Clinton, much less prevent her from facing trial.

If Trump is indicted or charged with criminal violations, and faces real jail time, do you think President Joe Biden will pardon him? Recall that Biden has rejected every effort by Trump to prevent disclosure of his White House records under a laughable claim of executive privilege. At the end of the day, it most likely won't matter who ignored subpoenas or relied on the Fifth Amendment to avoid answering questions. Truth has a way of coming out through all obstacles thrown in its path.

Trump has blasted everyone who has called for him to be held accountable for his actions. He has insulted and kicked to the curb those who defended him, until that burden became too much to bear. He maligned those who disagree with him. And he continues his doubling down ways to the present. Only those in Congress who have to be looking over their shoulders worried about their January 6 culpability, and his loyal base which may shrink as time moves on, remain in his corner.

If Trump is indicted, prosecuted and convicted, he will be on his own.

Oh, the irony of ironies!!

WHAT IS A PATRIOT?

Look at how Trump and his acolytes conflate words. A patriot is a person who vigorously supports his/her country and is prepared to defend it against enemies or detractors.

What Trump has done in denouncing the election as a fraud, and investigations of him as a witch hunt or hoax, is to equate himself with the country. To him, he is the country, and those who support him support the country. And by extension, the country it its people. Therefore, those who deny him are denying the country and its people; hence, they are "enemies of the people." This is the classic wordplay of an authoritarian. They do this with other words as well, such as freedom, liberty, justice, etc., using these words to define the behavioral opposite. This, of course, becomes dangerous when the masses buy into this.

WOULD YOU RATHER BE "WOKE" OR IGNORANT?

The definition of "woke" is to be aware of social injustices; to be informed. To be against this is to favor ignorance; and if people are ignorant, they repeat history's harsh mistakes. This kind of legislation must be taken to the courts; we still have a strong First Amendment, no matter how hard the right wing wants to water it down.

If these anti-woke folks had their way, all talk would be Happy Talk. No criticism of Republican officeholders. Everything would be taught with happy faces. Thinking would be prohibited. Actual knowledge and wisdom would be relegated to the back bench, or removed as being psychologically uncomfortable. Just a "Don't Worry, Be Happy" world for all of us. And we know what happens when ignorance supplants knowledge and wisdom.

HOW THE REPUBLICANS WORK THEIR GAME PLAN

Here's how this version of the Republican Party works. It says it stands for less government, less taxes and freedom. This all sounds so good, but in reality, it's only words. The party is, in reality, an empty suit. Ask a Republican why he or she likes the party, and they'll typically respond in the negative; that is, well, they'll stop America from becoming Socialist; the radical left will lead us to Communism and the Republicans will stop that; etc. Nothing positive. In short, the Republican Party is based on creating fear of the Democrats. In creating fear in the minds of their supporters, they evidently have no problem embracing Fascism or other forms of authoritarianism. The Trumpites--and there are millions of them---embrace Putin and dismiss Democratically elected officials. The Republicans favor huge tax breaks for the wealthy and increased taxes on certain groups in order to pay for those tax breaks; I could go on and on. It's easier to be swayed by the Republicans because anger and resentment is easier to arouse than having to actually think about and deal with substantive issues that the Democrats propose. The Democrats are policy oriented; the Republicans are oriented toward fear mongering. That's the key.

UH OH, HERE WE GO AGAIN

Here is a classic example of ignoring history at our peril.

Several far-right Republican House members plan to form an America First group, harking back to former President Trump's inaugural pledge of 2017. This should be met with a huge uh oh, here we go again.

A bit of history here. In 1940, the America First Committee (AFC) was formed. It was the foremost United States isolationist pressure group against American entry into World War II. Launched on September 4, the committee principally supported isolationism for its own sake, but many communists made use of the AFC, as well as antisemitic and pro-fascist speakers, who became its leaders.

Supported by Charles Lindbergh, among others, AFC membership peaked at 800,000 paying members in 450 chapters, making the AFC one of the largest antiwar organizations in the history of the United States. In fact, following a speech delivered by Lindbergh less than two months before Pearl Harbor, Wendell Willkie, the GOP presidential nominee, called it one of the most un-American speeches given by anyone with a national reputation, and many commentators, including journalists, said Lindbergh was pro-Nazi.

The committee was dissolved on December 10, 1941, three days after the attack on Pearl Harbor brought the United States into the war.

At the time Franklin Roosevelt declared war on Japan, and following reciprocal declarations of war involving Germany, America was not ready to wage war, largely because of the isolationist Congress and general mood of the country. It took Pearl Harbor to bring America into the war and put an end to isolationism. And it took the greatest mobilization of America's might to eventually win the war.

History teaches us how FDR, hampered by congressional isolationists, had to stand idly by while Hitler succeeded in invading a succession of European countries beginning in the mid-1930s.

Does this ring a bell after yesterday's invasion of Ukraine by Russia?

INCREDIBLE IGNORANCE

What amazes me is the tens of millions who still believe the Republican Party is the party of less government (telling folks what they can say and can't say in schools, colleges and universities, etc.), freedom and liberty (intruding into the privacy rights of women, telling us what books we can't read, telling folks how to sue local governments, etc.), less taxes (proposing tax increases on certain groups so the right wing can fund huge tax breaks for their large corporate cronies, or oligarchs), law and order (like assaulting law enforcement officers at the Capitol, ignoring investigative subpoenas, preventing public access to official records, destroying public presidential records, and calling the capital assault an exercise of legitimate political discourse, etc.) and their all-time favorite, family values (doing all of the above, while engaging in gaslighting of COVID and racial, ant-Semitic, and ethnic bias.

OUR "BETTER ANGELS" HAD BETTER APPEAR VERY SOON BEFORE THE CRISIS GETS OUT OF HAND

In his first inaugural address, President Abraham Lincoln called upon the better angels of our nature. As war clouds loomed over our country, he expressed hope that the people would rise above emotions and do what was right and best for our nation, encouraging them to emulate those who came before by answering the call to action.

Judging from events both domestic and foreign, we need those better angels now. Time is not on our side.

Domestically, as President Biden seeks universal condemnation of Russia's dictator Vladimir Putin for invading Ukraine, rather than voice support for actions taken, the usual band of extreme right-wing members of Congress, echoing their hero former President Donald Trump, have criticized Biden as being weak and corrupt, and unfit for office. You know their names: Sens. Ted Cruz,

Ron Johnson and Tom Cotton; and Reps. Elise Stefanik, Marjorie Taylor Greene, Matt Gaetz, Lauren Boebert, Andy Biggs and Paul Gosar. (Some of these have personal problems of their own, but of course that doesn't stop them from spilling their bile every chance they get.)

It seems that this band of radicals isn't bothered by undermining the president and his efforts to avoid a world war. And it's equally they're not bothered by the prospect of giving aid and comfort to Putin at a time of a potential world crisis stemming from the worst attack in Europe since World War II. For them, it's all about stirring up their base.

Where were these folks when Trump couldn't bend over far enough to kiss Putin's, ah, ring in Helsinki a few years ago? You remember when the FBI, our FBI, concluded that Putin interfered in the 2016 presidential election by helping Trump get elected. Well, of course Putin denied any such chicanery. Trump thus had to choose between the FBI and Putin. Trump infamously said "I believe him." These right-wing zealots obviously forgot about this little episode of weakness; their leader fawning over the words of a dictator and kicking the FBI to the curb. There are other examples of Trump's sellout to Putin, but to them, Trump is a pillar of strength, while Biden is weak.

But such is the case in the right-wing's topsy turvy Alice-in-Wonderland world of newspeak.

Meanwhile, on the foreign front, China's dictator XI Jinping has jumped to Putin's side, blaming the US-led NATO for creating tensions that forced his fellow dictator's hand. No doubt Xi is looking toward Taiwan. Can't have these countries that support democracy so close to absolute dictators. The people in Russia and China might learn about how these other countries live, and they might just like the idea of democratic freedoms.

I suppose that with NATO consisting of 30 countries with a total population of almost one billion, Putin might feel a bit jumpy. But he has now incurred the wrath of those countries, and his threats, while taken seriously, will not dissuade NATO, the UN, and other peace-keeping countries from condemning and isolating Putin. Millions of Russians will soon feel the effects of sanctions. How they will react will be most telling.

Here is Putin's problem with China. In the world of megalomania, there is room for only one king, emperor, Caesar, etc. Putin wants to be that one; so does Xi. And in a den of thieves, there is no honor. Sooner or later, these power-hungry types turn on one another.

Stay tuned.